# Unification of Tort Law: Wrongfulness

—

# Unification of Tort Law: Wrongfulness

H. Koziol (Editor)
F. D. Busnelli/G. Commandé
H. Cousy
K. D. Kerameus
J. Neethling
W. V. H. Rogers
J. Spier
G. Viney
P. Widmer

KLUWER LAW
INTERNATIONAL
THE HAGUE – LONDON – BOSTON

*Published by Kluwer Law International*
P.O. Box 85889
2508 CN The Hague, The Netherlands

*Sold and distributed in the USA and Canada by*
Kluwer Law International
675 Massachusetts Avenue
Cambridge, MA 02139, USA

*Sold and distributed in all other countries by*
Kluwer Law International
Distribution Centre
P.O. Box 322
3300 AH Dordrecht, The Netherlands

**Library of Congress Cataloging–in–Publication Data**

Unification of tort law : wrongfulness / edited by Helmut Koziol
        p.   cm. - - (Principles of European tort law ; v. 3)
        Includes index.
        ISBN 9041110194 (hardbound : alk. paper)
        1.  Torts--Europe.        I. koziol , Helmut.  II. Series.
    KJC1640 . U55   1998
    346 . 403--dc21                                    98 - 20268


This book is published with the financial support of the Verein der Freunde der Rechts– und Staatswissenschaftlichen Fakultät der Universität Wien.


*Printed on acid-free paper*

ISBN: 90 411 1019 4


© 1998 Kluwer Law International

Kluwer Law International incorporates the publishing programmes of Graham & Trotman Ltd., Kluwer Law and Taxation Publishers and Martinus Nijhoff Publishers

# Contents

# Introduction

# Introduction

Helmut Koziol

In 1993 the Dutchman Jaap Spier (University of Tilburg) called into being a group of tort lawyers. At first these scholars dealt with the limits of liability[1] and they applied the results to specific cases and drafted some comparative reports.[2] Afterwards the group decided to embark on the drafting of Principles of European Tort Law. We thought it to be the best proceeding to start one after another with discussing the most relevant factors in establishing liability such as wrongfulness, causation, damage, fault and the area of strict liability. The next steps will be the coordination of the results, the supplementation of other important factors and a first overall draft.

The group – usually called the 'Tilburg-Group' – decided to begin discussions with the topic 'wrongfulness'. At this stage members of the group were Jaap Spier (Tilburg) as leader, Christian von Bar (Osnabrück), Francesco Busnelli (Pisa), Herman Cousy (Leuven), Dan B. Dobbs (Tucson), Bill W. Dufwa (Stockholm), Michael G. Faure (Maastricht), Olav Haazen (Tilburg), Konstantinos D. Kerameus (Athens), Helmut Koziol (Vienna), Johann Neethling (Pretoria), Jorge Sinde Monteiro (Coimbra), W.V. Horton Rogers (Leeds), Gary T. Schwartz (Los Angeles), Geneviève Viney (Paris), Pierre Widmer (Lausanne), Michael Will (Geneva). We thought that the most promising way would be to combine theoretical abstract analysis with the discussion of concrete cases. Therefore, firstly every member was asked to write a report on wrongfulness under her or his legal system, especially working out its concept and its importance in establishing liability. Secondly, thirteen cases had to be considered.

The vast majority of the members holds the opinion that principles on European tort law should be very *flexible*. Taking this into account a general clause seems to be the best solution. It would also be a relatively easy way: e.g., following the English example[3] it could be stated that a person behaves wrongfully if she or he does not act as a reasonable

---

1   *See* J. Spier (Ed.), *The Limits of Liability. Keeping the Floodgates Shut* (1996), The Hague, Kluwer Law International.
2   J. Spier (Ed.), *The Limits of Expanding Liability* (1998), The Hague, Kluwer Law International.
3   *Cf. Winfield & Jolowicz on Tort* (14th ed. 1994), by W.V.H. Rogers, p. 125 f.

3

*H. Koziol (ed.), Unification of Tort Law: Wrongfulness,* 3-4.
©1998 *Kluwer Law International. Printed in The Netherlands.*

man would do. But all the supreme courts would understand the general clause rather differently according to their legal system up to the new European tort law and by that a unification would not be within reach. Therefore, the majority of the group also thinks it indispensable that the principles are drafted as *precisely* as possible and with sufficient determination. Both goals can probably only be reached by a flexible system.[4] This system makes it possible to take into consideration all the factors to which importance is attached in the different legal systems. Furthermore, by providing judges with as many relevant factors in establishing wrongfulness as possible and by laying down the rich experience of many legal systems, the judges' burden would be eased considerably and the courts' decisions would be foreseeable to a higher degree. As a preparation, some members tried to work out the nature of the protected interests and the important reasons for the extent of protection.

Finally, we thought it useful to begin the discussion on the borderline between contractual and tortious liability. In this area it will be also necessary to coordinate our draft with that of those groups who are working on principles of European law of obligations.

Our group was of the opinion that in this phase of our work we should not publish our draft on principles of wrongfulness as at first we want to get an overview of the most important factors in establishing liability. But we thought it useful for other scholars to get some information on wrongfulness in other legal systems. Unfortunately, among others we received no paper for publication under German law, but I shall try to fill this gap to some extent in the Conclusions at the end of this book.

---

4    *Cf.* Wilburg, *Entwicklung eines beweglichen Systems im bürgerlichen Recht* (1950); F. Bydlinski, *Juristische Methodenlehre und Rechtsbegriff* (2nd ed. 1991), p. 529 ff.

# The Cases

## Case 1

P is a hairdresser in a small town. The wife of D, a banker, leaves him to live with P. D opens a hairdressing salon next door to P, ruthlessly undercutting his prices. After six months P goes bankrupt. D then immediately closes down his salon.

## Case 2

X, a diva, is engaged by P to sing at Covent Garden for a three-month season and to sing nowhere else during that period. D, the proprietor of Drury Lane, persuades X on the first day of the engagement to come and sing for him instead. X is not worth suing for damages.

## Case 3

Two 'parties' (X and Y) compete for a contract with A. It is agreed with A that the first one to arrive at A's office will get the contract. The 'parties' are neighbours. X leaves half a minute earlier than Y. On the way to A there is one traffic light, which is red. X stops. Y ignores the signal, in breach of a traffic statute. He therefore arrives first at A's office and gets the contract. Can X sue Y in tort, claiming breach of a statutory duty or any other ground?

It has to be assumed that X and Y did not enter into (a kind of) contractual relationship.

## Case 4

P supplies oil by pipeline to Ruritania, a province of Arcadia. Ruritania rebels and Arcadian legislation forbids all oil supply to the rebel province. D, by covert means, supplies oil to the rebels. As a result, the rebellion lasts six months longer than would otherwise have been the case, depriving P of oil revenues during this period. No private international law issues arise and the law of Arcadia is the same as yours.

## Case 5

A Minister has power to refer take-overs to a fair trading commission if he deems it in the public interest to do so. P and D are bitter rivals in a take-over battle for a famous department store. D makes dishonest representations to the minister about his business background and these convince the minister not to intervene. D wins the battle. Later the truth about D's background is discovered. Had the minister known this he would have referred the bid to P, but nothing can now be done. P was the only other bidder.

## Case 6

A had been in prison for a long time for financial fraud. He was completely rehabilitated. Fifteen years later, he made a career and reached the position of director of a private bank. From the official sources, it is impossible to discover A's criminal past.

B publishes in a newspaper a comment on A, mentioning his criminal history. The crime of fraud is so irreconcilable with A's position, that he realizes that he has to step down.

Can A sue B, given that the statement is entirely correct?

## Case 7

P, a former employee of D, applies for a job with X and requests a reference from D. D states in the reference that P's continual absence on the grounds of trivial illness makes him an unreliable employee. This is not a defensibly accurate view of P. As a result of the reference, X rejects P. Please disregard the (post) contractual obligations.

## Case 8

Two doctors of medicine are having dinner in a smart restaurant. They drink two-thirds of a bottle of Chablis (premier cru), then reject it. They also drink two-thirds of a bottle of Meursault, then reject it and subsequently drink some glasses of cognac. They enjoy the food, with the exception of an oyster, which is rejected.

Subsequently, they ask for the bill, which is very high ($500) and includes the two bottles of wine. There is a small argument about payment for the wine. This issue is not clearly solved between the owner of the restaurant and the diners, who leave shortly afterwards. They pay the whole amount (including the wine). However, they put the money under a plate where it is hardly visible.

Upon reaching the door, the owner believes that they are leaving without paying. He tries to stop one of them (V). V turns and makes a gesture with his arm, which is apparently interpreted as aggression. The owner pushes V (who has drunk quite a lot) slightly, as a result of which he falls against the door frame. V suffers severe personal injury.

Can V sue the owner of the restaurant?

Please disregard the (possible) consequences of an agreement between V and the owner.

## Case 9

An oil refinery (O) produces not only oil products but also a severely nasty smell. There is no statute against producing the smell.

Three neighbours (A, B and C) claim that they suffer damage, notably: A absolutely hates the smell; B gets a headache from it, C says that the value of his house diminished.

What if:
(a) O has a legally valid permit to do so;
(b) O does not have such a permit.

Can A, B or C sue O and if so, why?

## Case 10

(a) D is walking along the street and sees a blind person approaching an unfenced hole. D does nothing to prevent the blind man falling in.

(b) D lawfully digs a hole in the public road and fences it securely. Later, he receives information that vandals have removed the fence. D takes no steps. Later that night, P falls into the hole.

(c) A passing doctor (D) is asked by P to assist, but although it is clear that P is seriously injured, D refuses, because he is late for the cinema. P dies. Had he received treatment, he would have lived.

## Case 11

D offers P a data processing system for his business. P accepts the offer and enters into an arrangement with a programmer. After delivery of the computer, it turns out that it is unsuitable. P has to pay the programmer, although he can not do his work, and P suffers a drop in sales until he gets a suitable data processing system.

## Case 12

(a) D sells a dog to P. When P brushes the dog for the first time, it bites him badly. D did not tell P that the dog had a sore place that must not be brushed.

(b) Due to lack of agreement the contract of sale is void.

## Case 13

Nurse D gives P an injection. P falls ill because the medicine was three times more concentrated than it should have been. The medicine was wrongly labelled.

# Country Reports

# Austria

WRONGFULNESS UNDER AUSTRIAN LAW

Helmut Koziol

## I. General

*A. Unlawfulness is Legally Acknowledged as an Element Relevant for Liability*

'Unlawfulness' or 'wrongfulness' is explicitly mentioned by § 1294 ABGB (General Civil Code). This rule distinguishes between causation of damage by an unlawful act or omission on the one hand and by coincidence on the other hand. Moreover, § 1294 ABGB clearly states that fault requires unlawful behaviour. Fault is understood as an attitude; it is based on the personal accusation of 'defective' will. Since the ABGB in §§ 1295 ff. links liability to the existence of fault, unlawfulness plays an important role under Austrian tort law.

*B. The Importance of Unlawfulness in Establishing Liability*

The point of departure has to be that a person can only be liable for compensation if he himself or his sphere caused the harm of another person. But causation in and of itself can not lead to liability of the malefactor: since in principle each individual has to bear his loss himself (*cf.* § 1311 first sentence ABGB), there must be additional reasons to justify that another person has to compensate the damage. These reasons are called '*Zurechnungsgründe*' (elements establishing liability).[1]

Objective unlawfulness is one of the most important elements establishing liability. Jointly with fault, unlawfulness is the foundation of the essential and acknowledged heart of tort law, namely liability based on the fault of the tortfeasor (*cf.* §§ 1295, 1311 ABGB). But unlawfulness is also important in the area of vicarious liability. This responsibility requires behaviour of the servant which is contrary to the duties of the principal to the injured person or contrary to the duties towards all individuals.

---

1     As to the following, *see* Wilburg, *Die Elemente des Schadensrechts* (1941); F. Bydlinski, *System und Prinzipien des Privatrechts* (1996), p. 185 ff.

*H. Koziol (ed.), Unification of Tort Law: Wrongfulness*, 11–23.

Apart from that, unlawfulness can establish liability in combination with other reasons, especially with the '*wirtschaftlichen Tragfähigkeit*' (financial capacity to bear the damage). For example, persons under fourteen years of age and insane persons as a rule are not responsible for tortious acts, but the judge is allowed to impose on such persons liability without fault if they act unlawfully and if consideration of the financial situation of both the wrongdoer and the injured person speaks in favour of liability (§ 1310 ABGB). § 1306a ABGB corresponds to this rule and applies if someone causes harm in an emergency situation. Furthermore, § 6 *Mediengesetz* (media law) takes into account the financial situation.

In another wide area of liability, that is strict liability, heightened dangerousness of a lawful activity takes the place of the element of unlawfulness.[2] The crucial thought here is that the one who – within the accepted limits – uses an especially dangerous thing for his own purposes has to be answerable for the harm caused by it.

In the area of vicarious liability in tort (§ 1315 ABGB), the dangerousness of the sphere of the principal plays an important role in addition to unlawfulness:[3] The principal is responsible for harm caused by his incompetent or dangerous servant. The lack of aptitude creates a special source of danger.

According to the EC Directive, a new principle for liability was introduced into the Austrian legal system in the area of product liability. The strict liability of the producer cannot be explained solely by the greater degree of dangerousness, since the majority of products are not particularly dangerous. However, the deciding factor here is that, for the sake of economy, in the production of consumer goods the demands on safety and quality are not as high as they could be. As a result, the consumer who is injured by a defective product would have to bear the disadvantage, whereas all the other consumers would be the beneficiaries since they could acquire the products at a good price. The result, namely that one individual has to bear the risk and many other have the benefit, does not seem appropriate. It is much more reasonable that all consumers form a community of risk and jointly bear the harm. This goal can be reached by passing on the loss of the consumer to the producers and from them to all consumers in the form of higher prices.[4]

A certain affinity to the strict liability based on dangerousness can be found in the '*Eingriffshaftung*' (*cf.* § 364a ABGB, liability for damage caused by an officially licensed plant):[5] if someone is allowed not only to endanger others, but also to cause damage consciously, he has to compensate the harm caused by the enterprise. This thus makes up for the fact the others were deprived of their right of defence.

---

2    *Cf.* Canaris, 'Die Gefährdungshaftung im Lichte der neueren Rechtsentwicklung', JBl 1995, 2.
3    *Cf.* Bydlinski, *System und Prinzipien des Privatrechts* (1996), p. 212 ff.
4    *Cf.* Koziol, *Grundfragen der Produktehaftung* (1980), p. 58 f.
5    *Cf.* Rummel, *Ersatzansprüche bei summierten Immissionen* (1969), p. 76 ff.

## C. Determination of Unlawfulness

### 1. 'Verhaltensunrechtslehre' and 'Erfolgsunrechtslehre'

In Austria, '*Verhaltensunrechtslehre*' (theory of unlawfulness of conduct) is the dominant theory:[6] according to this doctrine, unlawfulness depends on the violation of a '*Verhaltensgebot*', i.e., a duty of care. Thus, the judgement of unlawfulness always relates to a human act itself and is based on a lack of care. Under Austrian law the '*Erfolgsunrechtslehre*' (theory of unlawfulness established by the result) is therefore rejected.

The '*Erfolgsunrechtslehre*' takes the view that unlawfulness depends solely on the harmful result, i.e., the mere violation of protected interests determines unlawfulness. This doctrine stresses rightly that the legal system protects certain interests and that violation of these interests is undesirable by law. Without a doubt, this aspect is important for answering the question of whether the person whose interests are endangered has the right of self-defence and the grounds to take action to restrain interference.

But the '*Erfolgsunrechtslehre*' also provokes quite a few questions. First, liability for fault is based on an accusation against the tortfeasor. Therefore the behaviour of the tortfeasor is important and that indicates that unlawfulness has to be judged regarding the behaviour and not the result. Furthermore, only human behaviour violates the law, as rules of law apply solely to persons. Therefore, it seems more appropriate that only conduct and not the result of such conduct should be called unlawful. Secondly, the '*Erfolgsunrechtslehre*' provokes the question, which reproach can be made of the damaging party if it was as careful as one can possibly be. Thirdly, it has to be considered that even life, health or freedom, which enjoy protection on the highest level, are not protected against every violation. E.g., unlawfulness depends, *inter alia*, on whether the person who injured another had a right of self-defence (*cf.* Case 8). Furthermore, when the defendant caused harm to the reputation (*cf.* Case 6), it has to be considered whether the statement of the defendant was true, whether a need for information exists and whether the defendant acted according to the right of free expression of opinion. Therefore, we have to ask ourselves whether, even in cases of interference with absolute rights, the result merely indicates unlawfulness without actually establishing it. Even this is very dubious if the defendant did not interfere directly with the absolute right, but only indirectly. E.g., a variation of Case 13: a physician prescribes a medication in wrong quantity; the prescription was based on the leading textbook. In the case of indirect interference, the result can not be decisive. Finally, pure economic interests are protected only in some respects. Therefore, if the defendant causes pure economic loss, the result can not even be said to indicate unlawfulness.

On the other hand, very often the argument is used that there would be no difference between unlawfulness and fault if we accept the '*Verhaltensunrechtslehre*'. But I think this argument can not bring the '*Verhaltensunrechtslehre*' into disrepute: The yardstick for unlawfulness is an objective one and the yardstick for fault is subjective. For example: a minor or an insane person acts unlawfully if he does not observe the objective duties

---

6    *Cf.* Koziol, *Österreichisches Haftpflichtrecht* I (3rd ed. 1997), No. 4/1 ff.

of care, that is if he does not behave as a reasonable man should have. But because of his inability there is no fault.

Furthermore, one has to discuss the question whether the '*Verhaltensunrecht*' is necessary or at least useful. The combination of '*Erfolgsunrecht*' and fault seems to lead to the same results as '*Verhaltensunrecht*' and fault. But I do not think that this is true. Again, we have to consider damage caused by children or insane persons. Under Austrian law (§ 1310 ABGB), a minor must compensate damages on the condition that his behaviour was unlawful and that the financial position speaks in favour of liability; therefore, he is liable even though he acted without fault owing to his age. If the minor did not violate an objective duty of care and '*Erfolgsunrecht*' would be considered sufficient, the minor has to compensate on account of his financial situation whereas an adult would never be liable. Therefore, I think that the '*Erfolgsunrechtslehre*' does not give the decisive answer in cases where liability is based on unlawfulness but does not require fault.

Although '*Erfolgsunrechtslehre*' does not seem preferable, it stresses some useful aspects which are important in considering the right of self-defence and to take action to restrain interference. Therefore, I think that a sort of compromise would be the most reasonable solution.

The first step in trying to establish liability is to examine whether the defendant caused a result that our legal system seeks to prohibit. In German I would prefer to speak about '*Tatbildmäßigkeit*': at stake is whether the very abstract legal elements of a tort are given, e.g., if the physical integrity of a person is harmed. To put it another way: one has to ask if there is an interference of protected rights and interests. If there is interference with an absolute right, this can to some degree indicate that the behaviour is unlawful.

The second step should be to judge whether the defendant violated an objective duty of care described by law. It has to be stressed that the '*Verhaltensunrechtslehre*' is not only relevant if interference with protected interests has to be judged, but also if a protective law (*Schutzgesetz*) is violated. A *Schutzgesetz* calls for certain behaviour and, therefore, only conduct has to be judged. This puts forward a reason why unlawfulness is not established if the defendant did not act as the law demanded but behaved as carefully as a reasonable man was able to do.

In the area of liability based on fault, the third step has to be to investigate whether the defendant acted with subjective fault (negligence).

## 2. Establishing unlawfulness
The unlawfulness of conduct can be established, on the one hand, by the breach of a contractual duty of care.

On the other hand, under the law of torts a distinction has to be made. First of all, unlawfulness of conduct can be the result of violation of a particular imperative rule which forbids due to its abstract dangerousness conduct which is fairly precisely described. Such concrete imperative rules of conduct are called '*Schutzgesetze*' (protective laws, *cf.* § 1311 sentence 2 case 2 ABGB). The Road Traffic Regulations are a good illustration of this.

Furthermore, § 1295 subsection 2 ABGB provides that those persons behave unlawfully who are acting *contra bonos mores*[7] and wilfully inflict damage. Exactly which conduct is unlawful under this rule can not be established as easily as in the case of violating a protective rule. It seems to be true that unlawfulness is determined based on the personal unworthiness of the conduct; from this standpoint the purposeful behaviour carries weight.[8]

The legal system does not call for or forbid an exactly described behaviour in a very broad and important area. Here, the legal system only recognises protected positions by assigning rights or assets to a person and commanding all others to respect them. The scope of protection can be very wide, as is the case for traditional absolute rights, the endangering of which is prohibited in a very general way. But the legal system sometimes also acknowledges protection, which is much narrower. Thus, the scope of protection is laid down by describing certain interests and the more or less wide prohibition of endangering these interests.

But unlawfulness of a conduct which endangers these protected positions without authorization is given only if the behaviour also violates an objective duty of care.

## 3. Unlawfulness based on endangering protected spheres[9]

Far-reaching protection is granted to traditional absolute rights; these are especially rights of personality, rights *in rem* and intangible property rights. Common to all of these rights is that their content has reasonably clear contours, so that the protected sphere is discernible to third parties (*cf.* § 354 ABGB). Problems arise, however, regarding the situation in the area of rights of personality: the originally accepted rights are clearly outlined, e.g., the right to physical well being, to liberty, to bear a name. But now rights of personality, which are not precisely defined, are also accepted, e.g., the right to privacy. Some accept even a general right of personality. But it turns out that the protection is minor if the contours are ill-defined.[10]

Traditional absolute rights have still another important quality: they are obvious.[11] That means that third persons are aware of their existence and range. This is true as well

---

7    Regarding the term *contra bonos mores* ('*gute Sitten*') *cf.* Bydlinski, *Juristische Methodenlehre und Rechtsbegriff* (2nd ed. 1991), p. 495 f.; Koziol and Welser, *Grundriß des bürgerlichen Rechts* I (10th ed. 1995), p. 145 f. with further supporting documents.

8    Karollus, *Funktion und Dogmatik der Haftung aus Schutzgesetzverletzung* (1992), p. 51 f.

9    *Cf.* Koziol, 'Das niederländische BW und der Schweizer Entwurf als Vorbilder für ein künftiges europäisches Schadenersatzrecht', ZEuP 1996, 596 ff.; Schilcher and Posch, 'Civil Liability for Pure Economic Loss: An Austrian Perspective', in: Banakas (Ed.), *Civil Liability for Pure Economic Loss* (1996), p. 174 ff.

10   *Cf.* Canaris, 'Grundprobleme des privatrechtlichen Persönlichkeitsschutzes', JBl 1991, 208 ff.

11   Concerning the importance of obviousness *cf.* Fabricius, 'Zur Dogmatik des "sonstigen Rechts" gemäß § 823 Abs. I BGB', AcP 160 (1961), 273; Koziol, *Die Beeinträchtigung fremder Forderungsrechte* (1967), p. 174 ff.; Picker, 'Positive Forderungsverletzung und culpa in contrahendo – Zur Problematik der Haftung "zwischen" Vertrag und Delikt', AcP 183 (1983), 480 ff.; Larenz and Canaris, *Lehrbuch des Schuldrechts* II/2, Besonderer Teil (13th ed. 1994), § 76 I 1 b.

for traditional rights of personality, because the existence of the person and the content of the right are discernible. The obviousness is important for the protection, because it makes the protection of these rights all the more reasonable. Freedom of movement would be much more restricted if everyone had to reckon with sanctions as a result of violating an indiscernible right.

But one must not conclude from this that solely traditional absolute rights are protected by law.[12] It is precisely the personal rights which show us that the content of rights can be defined to various degrees and obviousness can also vary. But they are protected nevertheless. However, protection is minor if the content is not clearly defined or obviousness is not given.

If a legal position is not obvious, general protection is out of the question. But knowledge in a particular case has to be treated as equal to obviousness.[13] Thus, the protection of such legal positions is restricted: they must be respected only by those persons who know them. This is the reason why interference in contractual relations is only illegal if the third party is aware of the contract.[14] Protection is minimal if contours are not clear and obviousness is not given; therefore pure economic loss only rarely has to be compensated.

But acknowledgement of the protection of a sphere not only depends on clearness of contours and obviousness or knowledge. As every protected sphere means restriction of freedom of movement to all others, acknowledgement of protection requires, in a very abstract sense, balancing the interests of the person who needs protection and those of third parties.[15] The traditional personal rights of personality, such as the rights to life, physical well-being or liberty, rank highest.

As each of the above-mentioned factors can be of varying strengths, they are often only able to establish a protected sphere in combination with a very weighty factor or with several factors. Furthermore, the scope of the protection depends on the total weight of the factors.

By the same token, the answer to the question, 'Which specific behaviour is illegal?' requires the weighing of all the interests. The fact that a third party interferes with a protected sphere is an absolute prerequisite for discussing illegality. But on its own it is not enough to establish unlawfulness, because in order to do so, in the concrete situation the interfering person must have violated an objective duty to take care.

Here again, the value of the endangered protected positions (e.g., the rights to physical well-being and ownership) and the significance of the menacing interference are important; these have to be evaluated relative to the interest of third parties to exercise their freedom of movement. For example, if endangering life is at stake, restriction of freedom of behaviour of third parties is reasonable to a greater degree than in cases where only objects are endangered.

---

12  As expounded by Karollus, *Funktion und Dogmatik der Haftung aus Schutzgesetzverletzung* (1992), p. 46 ff.
13  *Cf.* Koziol, *Die Beeinträchtigung fremder Forderungsrechte* (1967), p. 178 ff.
14  *See* on this subject Koziol, *Österreichisches Haftpflichtrecht* II (2nd ed. 1984), p. 40 ff.
15  *Cf.* Picker, 'Vertragliche und deliktische Schadenshaftung', JZ 1987, 1052.

Another important aspect is to which extent the conduct is apt to cause damage.[16] The greater the danger of a behaviour, the more diligence has to be demanded.[17] One has to take into account that even behaviour that is not very dangerous in general can gain a very high degree of dangerousness if the conduct is done with the intent of causing harm.[18]

But the dangerousness of a conduct for a protected sphere is not necessarily sufficient on its own to establish unlawfulness: the interest of the third party in exercising the dangerous behaviour must also be considered.[19] This shows the area in which strict liability is given: in spite of high aptness of the conduct to cause damage, driving a car is not prohibited. The same thought is relevant in establishing the right to act in self-defence.

Finally, we have to take into consideration the burden (costs) of avoiding endangering an individual and the reasonableness of such costs.[20]

## D. Unlawfulness and Fault

On the basis of prevailing opinion in Austria, a very clear distinction can be made between unlawfulness and fault: only objective factors are decisive in determining unlawfulness. Therefore, a general standard must be applied in answering the question of which conduct is reasonable. On the other hand, fault is understood as a 'defect' of will and has to be judged by considering the individual abilities of the defendant.[21] Thus, not every unlawful behaviour is automatically culpable. The difference can be best demonstrated by the example of a tortfeasor who is mentally ill: his conduct can be unlawful but as a rule it is not culpable (*cf.* § 1310 ABGB).

But in Austria the difference is stressed even apart from such obvious cases, because general opinion holds that fault has to be judged on the basis of a subjective standard. It is decisive if, on account of his individual abilities, an actual tortfeasor was able to recognize the unlawfulness of his conduct as well as the occurrence of damage and behave according to law. To accuse someone personally of having a 'defect' of will is

---

16  For a comprehensive analysis, *see* Münzberg, *Verhalten und Erfolg als Grundlagen der Rechtswidrigkeit und Haftung* (1966), p. 141 ff.; and before him Wilburg, *Die Elemente des Schadensrechts* (1941), p. 44. *Cf.* Deutsch, 'Gefahr, Gefährdung, Gefahrerhöhung', *Larenz-FS* (1983), p. 897; U. Huber, 'Verschulden, Gefährdung und Adäquanz', *Wahl-FS* (1973), p. 305 ff.; Widmer, 'Gefahren des Gefahrensatzes', ZBJV 1970, 302 ff.

17  *Cf.* Koziol, 'Bewegliches System und Gefährdungshaftung', in: Bydlinski, Krejci, Schilcher and Steininger (Ed.), *Das Bewegliche System im geltenden und künftigen Recht* (1986), p. 53, with further supporting documents. *Cf.* also Mayer-Maly, 'Plädoyer für einen Abschied von der Gefahrengeneigtheit', *Hilger und Stumpf-FS* (1983), p. 467.

18  Reischauer in: Rummel, *Kommentar zum Allgemeinen bürgerlichen Gesetzbuch* II, (2nd ed. 1992), § 1294 No. 12 and Karollus, *Funktion und Dogmatik der Haftung aus Schutzgesetzverletzung* (1992), p. 205 ff., p. 212 f., say rightly that this is a subjective factor of unlawfulness.

19  In this sense OGH in SZ 26/255.

20  *Cf.* Gimpel-Hinteregger, *Grundfragen der Umwelthaftung* (1994), p. 96.

21  *Cf.* Koziol, 'Objektivierung des Fahrlässigkeitsmaßstabes im Schadenersatzrecht?', AcP 196 (1996), 593.

only possible if his individual capacity was sufficient to avoid the interference. Only then can it be said that he acted with fault.

Regarding the degree of the required attention and diligence, an objective standard must always be applied. One has to summon up ordinary attention and diligence (§§ 1294, 1297 ABGB).

It should be mentioned that the liability of experts presents an exception:[22] according to § 1299 ABGB, their fault has to be judged by an objective standard – even regarding knowledge and ability. Thus, everyone who carries out a profession that demands special abilities has to guarantee that he has the necessary capacities.

## II. The Cases

### A. Case 1

By opening a competing business and by undercutting prices, D caused pure economic loss to P. Interference with pure economic interests of other persons is only unlawful under strict conditions.[23] The limited protection of pure economic interests goes back to the fact that what is at stake is not a separate and obvious position which has clearly contoured content and which is in principle acknowledged by law as a protected sphere. Thus, on the one hand, the interests of the owner of the property do not rank highest, and, on the other hand, the freedom of movement of third parties would be seriously restricted by protecting such interests, as interference could easily creep in.[24] The low ranking of the property owners interests has the consequence that even damage by intent is not unlawful if the tortfeasor pursues approved interests. As the example of fair competition shows, these interests do not have to rank higher than those of the injured party.

Still, pure economic interests are protected by § 1295 subsection 2 ABGB, which bans behaviour that is *contra bonos mores*. Moreover, it has to be assumed that prejudice of pure economic interests is always unlawful if the interests of the tortfeasor rank much lower than those of the owner of property and if the tortfeasor acts with intent to cause damage (*cf.* §§ 874, 1300 ABGB).[25]

In the case under consideration, D causes damage to P not for the sake of fair competition, which is approved by law, but rather for the sake of revenge. Thus, the behaviour of D can possibly be qualified as *contra bonos mores*, which would consequently make it unlawful. Regardless of this, the conduct is unlawful in any case, because the interests of D rank much lower than the interests of P.

---

22 *Cf.* Welser, *Die Haftung für Rat, Auskunft und Gutachten* (1983), p. 23 ff.; OGH in JBl 1993, 389.

23 OGH in SZ 66/77; ÖBA 1994, 73 and 400; Karollus, *Funktion und Dogmatik der Haftung aus Schutzgesetzverletzung* (1992), p. 43 ff.; Koziol, 'Generalnorm und Einzeltatbestände als Systeme der Verschuldenshaftung: Unterschiede und Angleichungsmöglichkeiten', ZEuP 1995, 359.

24 *See* in this sense Karollus, *Funktion und Dogmatik der Haftung aus Schutzgesetzverletzung* (1992), p. 48 f.

25 *Cf.* Koziol, *Österreichisches Haftpflichtrecht* II (2nd ed. 1984), p. 21.

## B. Case 2

Under Austrian law it is commonly accepted that third parties act unlawfully if they are aware of a contract and nevertheless induce the debtor to breach it.[26] This point of view is based on the following consideration: on the one hand, the creditor has a reasonable interest in the protection of his position, which is accepted by law, and, in principle, the legal system has to see to it that third parties do not interfere whenever they like with such positions. On the other hand, contractual relations are not obvious to third parties; even less obvious are the very different contents. Thus, a general protection would restrict the freedom of movement of third parties to an unreasonable extent, as they would be forced to investigate the existence of a contract and as they would have to constantly expect claims from defence of creditors or liability for interference in contractual relations.

But it is not expecting too much of third parties, if it is a prerequisite for the protection of contracts that the third party knows the contract and if only intentional interference in the contractual relation is prohibited. The latter restriction also results from the fact that psychological causation is at stake and, in connection with this, generally only intentional influence is prohibited.[27]

## C. Case 3

Y does not observe the road traffic regulations and therefore definitely acts unlawfully. But the violated statute only intends to protect health and property of other road users, not pure economic interests.[28] Therefore, the loss of X lies outside the protective purpose of the law.

But I think Y also behaves unlawfully, because in a competitive situation he tries to gain a lead over X by using unfair means. Therefore, his behaviour has to be regarded as contrary to honest practices and is therefore unlawful (*cf.* § 1 UWG [Unfair Competition Act]).

## D. Case 4

D acts unlawfully, because he violates Arcadian oil supply legislation. But this law probably only intends to protect the interests of Arcadia, namely the suppression of the rebellion in Ruritania. Therefore, I assume that the loss of P is not included in the protective purpose of this law.

It is very doubtful whether D violates a duty of care towards P, as D only causes pure economic loss. The argument that D commits an act of unfair competition is perhaps not true in this case, as it seems that D did not act on reasons of competition, but rather to support the rebels. Furthermore, the loss of P was not directly caused by the oil supply,

---

26  OGH in SZ 55/170; JBl 1991, 719; JBl 1992, 704; RdW 1994, 242; Koziol, *Die Beeinträchtigung fremder Forderungsrechte* (1967).
27  *Cf.* Koziol, *Österreichisches Haftpflichtrecht* I, No. 4/52 ff.
28  OGH in JBl 1972, 268; SZ 44/16; SZ 50/34; ZVR 1979/93.

which could be qualified as an act of competition, but rather only by the prolongation of the rebellion. If the loss of P is attributed to the extension of the rebellion by the rebels and the ban on oil-delivery by Arcadia, the damage of P is incurred by an independent decision of third parties, thus D only contributes a psychological cause of P's damage. Therefore, D would only be considered as behaving unlawfully if he acts with the intent to influence the will of the rebels and of the state bodies of Arcadia in order to cause damage to P (*cf.* Case 2).

## E. Case 5

D acts unlawfully, as he uses unfair means to gain an advantage over the competitor P. *Cf.* Case 3.

## F. Case 6

According to § 1330 subsection 2 ABGB, only the spreading of untrue statements is illegal. Injury by true statements can not be prosecuted on the basis of this rule of law. But the true accusation of a punishable act, for which the sentence is already served or remitted, is punishable according to § 113 StGB (Criminal Code). Therefore, the behaviour of B was unlawful and B is liable due to violating a protective law (§ 1311 ABGB).

Furthermore, the behaviour of B could be *contra bonos mores* (§ 1295 subsection 2 ABGB) and consequently unlawful, if B wilfully spreads prejudicial facts to inflict damage, although there was no justified interest on his part or on the part of the individual to whom the statement is addressed.

## G. Case 7

§ 1330 subsection 2 ABGB shows that those persons act unlawfully who spread untrue statements which endanger the credit standing, earning capacity or the professional advancement of another person, if in exercising due care they should have realised the incorrectness of the statement.

But liability is only established in the case of intent if the statement was not offered publicly and either the informer or the addressee had a justified interest in the information. A justified interest exists if the information is important for personal, social or economic relations.

## H. Case 8

In principle, careless behaviour which endangers the physical health of another person is unlawful. If the owner of the restaurant pushes V, who obviously is no longer steady, then he endangers the safety of V in an unlawful manner.

In the case in point, however, the owner wanted to avert danger; therefore, it has to be examined whether he can argue a legally recognized justification, namely the right of self-defence (§ 19 ABGB). The precondition for this right is that the owner defended himself against an unlawful attack of V. But the existence of this precondition is dubious: V defended himself against the attempt of the owner to prevent him from leaving the restaurant. As V had paid the bill, the owner was not entitled to restrict, in his own interests, the freedom of movement of V and so the owner acted unlawfully. Therefore V, as far as he is concerned, defended himself against an unlawful attack of the owner and his behaviour was not illegal. The owner of the restaurant had no right of self-defence against the lawful defence of V, so there is no justification. Therefore, the owner acted unlawfully by pushing V.

As V did not attack the owner in an illegal manner, the owner could only argue a putative right of self-defence. But this argument is only appropriate for rejecting the subjective fault.[29] The owner would be acting without fault if it was not recognizable to him that V had paid the bill, nor that V was therefore allowed to defend himself against the owner.

## I. Case 9

(a) If O has a permit to run the factory, the production of the smell is not unlawful, provided this is included by the permit.[30] But nevertheless, O could be liable on the basis of the '*Eingriffshaftung*' (§ 364a ABGB, *cf.* above under I.B.). But the claims of A, B and C depend on whether the nuisances caused by emissions from the neighbouring property exceed the customary degree in that place and considerably impede the customary use.

An exception has to be made to this principle if the emissions seriously endanger the health of persons: such emissions are not allowed under any circumstances.[31]

(b) If O's plant is not officially licensed, then all emissions which exceed the customary degree and considerably impede the customary use of the real property are not allowed.[32] If the emissions are of that quality, then O can be liable for fault (§ 364 ABGB).

## J. Case 10

(a) It is true that under Austrian law no general duty exists to protect other persons from damage.[33] But in a widely held opinion, D is acting unlawfully if he does not save P from

---

29  *Cf.* OGH in JBl 1967, 320; EvBl 1972/219.
30  *Cf.* OGH in SZ 50/84; EvBl 1983/82; Recht der Umwelt 1994, 152 with commentary by Kerschner.
31  Jabornegg, *Bürgerliches Recht und Umweltschutz* (1985), p. 67 ff.; Stabentheiner, 'Zivilrechtliche Unterlassungsansprüche zur Abwehr gesundheitsgefährdender Umwelteinwirkungen', ÖJZ 1992, p. 83 ff.; Gimpel-Hinteregger, *Grundfragen der Umwelthaftung* (1994), p.285.
32  *Cf.* Koziol and Welser, *Grundriß des bürgerlichen Rechts* I (10th ed. 1995), p. 42 f., with further supporting documents.
33  OGH in SZ 50/100.

serious injury, although he could have achieved the rescue easily and without endangering himself.[34]

(b)  As D established by his activity a source of potential danger, it is his duty to take steps to ensure the protection of other persons against the risks created by him (*'Verkehrssicherungspflicht'*). This rule is even applicable if the danger is provoked by third parties.[35]

(c)  In the case of misadventure, everyone has the duty to give such aid as is necessary to save the life or to avoid a high risk to the health of someone if it is not in conflict with his substantial interest.[36] Therefore, the passing doctor is liable.

## K. Case 11

On the one hand, D may be liable for breach of contract if, according to the contract, D should deliver a suitable computer. On the other hand, D may have acted wrongfully in the form of misrepresentation before entering into the contract. If he did not sufficiently inform P before the conclusion of the contract about the capacity of the computer, he may have acted unlawfully by violating obligations to give information.[37] The duty to give true and sufficient information is not a contractual obligation, but rather a duty prior to contract (*culpa in contrahendo*). This point of view is of special importance if, as a consequence of the misrepresentation, the contract only contains the obligation to deliver a certain computer without stipulating that said computer is sufficient for the client's purpose. It has to be stressed that the behaviour of D can be unlawful, although he only causes pure economic loss to P. Under Austrian law it is commonly accepted that, from the beginning of a business contact, special duties of care between the parties are established.[38] These duties are much more intensive than in the real field of tort law. Each partner has to take action to safeguard the other from harm and they also have the purpose of protecting pure economic interests. The reason for this is threefold. The contact establishes a special relationship with the partner; every partner has a greater possibility to endanger the sphere of the other partner; and the contact is in the interest of each partner.[39]

There is a difference regarding the damage caused by breach of contract and the damage caused by misrepresentation. That is why in the first case D has to compensate

---

34  Steininger, 'Schadenersatz wegen Unterlassens der Hilfeleistung bei Verkehrsunfällen', JBl 1961, 255; Koziol, *Österreichisches Haftpflichtrecht* I (3rd ed. 1997), No. 4/61; OGH in SZ 59/7; of dissenting opinion Reischauer in Rummel, ABGB § 1294, No. 3.

35  OGH in SZ 60/256.

36  *Cf.* § 95 StGB (Criminal Code); Mayer-Maly, 'Schädigung durch Unterlassung, insbesondere durch unterlassene Hilfeleistung bei Verkehrsunfällen', ZVR 1977, 99.

37  *Cf.* OGH in JBl 1992, 450; ÖBA 1993, 408 with commentary by Koch.

38  *Cf.* Welser, *Vertretung ohne Vollmacht* (1970); *ibid.*, 'Das Verschulden beim Vertragsabschluß im österreichischen Recht', ÖJZ 1973, 281.

39  *Cf.* Koziol, 'Delikt, Verletzung von Schuldverhältnissen und Zwischenbereich', JBl 1994, 217.

the interest of P in the performance of the contract, whereas in the second D has to compensate the loss incurred to P as a result of relying on untrue information.

## L. Case 12

(a) The duties of care, which are established from the beginning of a business contact, continue to exist after the conclusion of the contract. According to these duties the parties are also required to actively safeguard the other party from harm. Thus, for example, the seller is obliged to inform the buyer about the special dangerousness of the object of sale. Therefore D should have informed P about the special sensitiveness of the dog and the danger of caring for the dog.[40]

(b) Today it is commonly accepted that the special duties of care are established by business contact and do not require the conclusion of the contract. Therefore, the duties of care, especially the obligation to give information, exist even if the contract is not in effect:[41] even then there is a special proximity between the parties.

## M. Case 13

If the medicine was incorrectly labelled and if, even in exercising due care, the nurse was not able to recognize its dangerous concentration, then the nurse did not act unlawfully. This is a consequence of the '*Verhaltensunrechtslehre*' (*cf.* I.C.1.), the dominating theory under Austrian law: the judgement of unlawfulness is always based on an objective lack of care. Going by the '*Erfolgsunrechtslehre*', the answer would be different: according to this theory, unlawfulness is given, since P is injured, and only subjective fault is lacking.

---

40  *Cf.* Schlesinger, 'Das Wesen der positiven Vertragsverletzung', *Zentralblatt für die juristische Praxis* 1926, 721.
41  Koziol, *Österreichisches Haftpflichtrecht* II (2nd ed. 1984), p. 79 f.

# THE BORDERLINE BETWEEN TORT LIABILITY AND CONTRACT

## Helmut Koziol

Under Austrian law the question whether a claim can be based on contract or tort law is relevant in view of the onus of proof (§§ 1296, 1298 ABGB), vicarious liability (§§ 1313a, 1315 ABGB) and the extent of protection of pure economic interests. On the other hand, there is no difference in regard of limitation periods, contributory negligence, application of legal causation and compensation for immaterial damage.

Liability based on tort and liability based on breach of contract usually are taken as clearly separated contrasts. But I think that they are the two ends of liability based on fault and that between them there is a connecting chain of intermediate stages.[1] This understanding is important because one has not to sort liability in one of these two categories and, therefore, is able to avoid abruptly different treatment of rather similar cases.

In the result, this already has been done to some extent, e.g., by accepting special duties of care prior to conclusion of contract (*cf.* Case 11) and contracts with protective purpose in favour of third parties. But up to now, this start is not very satisfactory: on the one hand, only few special intermediate stages have been realized. On the other hand, they have been sorted in one of the two ends and, by that, they are not treated as intermediate stages but rigidly as breach of contract or as tortious act.

Regarding the area of unlawfulness the acknowledgement that there is no clear-cut dividing line between contractual and tortious liability is important for two reasons. First, under tort law duties of care to protect pure economic interests of other persons only exist in very narrow borders[2] whereas the partners of a contract are one another obliged to take care of pure economic interests. Secondly, the partners of a contract are one another bound to very extensive and severe duties of care. In particular, each partner has to take action to safeguard the other from harm, e.g., by giving true and sufficient information and warning.

The arguments for the different protection under tort law and under the law of contract are the following. More extensive duties of care under tort law would lead to an unreasonable restriction of freedom of action for all individuals. This would especially be true if one would accept far-reaching duties to take action. Besides, more severe duties of care to everybody would lead to a vast number of claimants and, by this, to

---

1    For more detail *see* Koziol, 'Delikt, Verletzung von Schuldverhältnissen und Zwischenbereich', JBl 1994, 209; *ibid.*, 'Generalnorm und Einzeltatbestände als Systeme der Verschuldenshaftung: Unterschiede und Angleichungsmöglichkeiten', ZEuP 1995, 363.

2    *Cf.* OGH in SZ 61/279; SZ 67/17 = JBl 1994, 687.

*H. Koziol (ed.), Unification of Tort Law: Wrongfulness, 25–27.*
©*1998 Kluwer Law International. Printed in The Netherlands.*

incalculable risks.[3] Furthermore, it has to be considered that the parties of a contract have much higher opportunity to cause harm to the person and the property of the partner and even to pure economic interests. The increased endangering calls for intensified duties of care. Finally, it is significant that in the area of contracts both parties pursue business interests.[4] If someone follows up his own business interests and by that endangers another person in a higher degree then higher duties of care are reasonable.[5]

The basic ideas for making a difference between tort and breach of contract are only true for the core of the respective area. But only some of the arguments apply in the vast intermediate area; and apart from that, the reasons can be given in full or less intensity. Therefore, one must accept that between the core of tort and the core of breach of contract there is no clear dividing line and they are connected by many links.[6] Exactly in this spirit Canaris[7] worked out liability for '*Schutzpflichtverletzungen*' (breach of special duties of care established by business contact) as '*dritte Spur*' (third lane) between liability based on tort and liability based on breach of contract. But he thinks it to be based on the fundamental idea of '*Vertrauenshaftung*' (liability for breach of trust) and, therefore, restricts it to the area of legal transaction. I think this restriction not justified because some of the reasons for severe liability for breach of contract are relevant even beyond this area and are suitable to tighten up liability, for instance in the area of mere social contact[8] (e.g., joint mountaineering[9]) or of neighbourhood.

If in the intermediate zone the interests are thus that, on the one hand, some valuations of tort law are relevant but, on the other hand, also some of contract law it would be not according to law to apply solely tort law or contract law. A solution according to statutory valuations has to combine the principles of both areas: depending on whether the basic ideas of one area or of the other area are more relevant and to what extent, the regulations solely of one of the areas or of a combination of the regulations of both areas have to be applied. I would like to illustrate this by some examples.

Next to the breach of contractual obligations of performance is the '*positive Forderungsverletzungen*'. This is a breach of an obligation other than by delay or impossibility, so a breach of special duties of care to the partner (*cf.* Case 12(a)). These duties of care exist independent of the validity of the contract (*cf.* Case 12(b)). Decisive is first, that there is a special relationship between the two parties and, therefore, one has

---

3    *See* also Picker, 'Positive Forderungsverletzung und culpa in contrahendo – Zur Problematik der Haftung "zwischen" Vertrag und Delikt', AcP 183 (1983), 476 ff.; *ibid.*, 'Vertragliche und deliktische Schadenshaftung', JZ 1987, 1052 ff., though he is overstressing this idea of limiting liability ignoring the other reasons for different liability.

4    *Cf.* Welser, *Vertretung ohne Vollmacht* (1970), p. 76 f.; F. Bydlinski, 'Zur Haftung der Dienstleistungsberufe in Österreich und nach dem EG-Richtlinienvorschlag', JBl 1992, 345.

5    *Cf.* Canaris, 'Schutzgesetz – Verkehrspflichten – Schutzpflichten', *Larenz-FS* (1983), p. 88.

6    This is accepted by the OGH in JBl 1995, 522 = ÖBA 1995, 986.

7    *Larenz-FS* (1983), p. 84 ff.; *cf.* also Medicus, 'Die culpa in contrahendo zwischen Vertrag und Delikt', *Max Keller-FS* (1989), p. 205.

8    *Cf.* Hoffmann, 'Der Einfluß des Gefälligkeitsmoments auf das Haftungsmaß', AcP 167 (1967), 400 f.

9    *Cf.* Michalek, *Die Haftung des Bergsteigers bei alpinen Unfällen*, (Diss. Wien 1990), p. 48 ff. Critical Galli, *Haftungsprobleme bei alpinen Tourengemeinschaften* (1995), p. 67 ff.

not to be afraid of an unreasonable extension of liability, even not for pure economic loss. Secondly, the parties of a contract, even of a void contract, have much higher opportunity to cause harm to the person of the partner, his property and his pure economic interests. Thirdly, each party tries to pursue his business interests. Therefore, even in case of invalidity of the contract the duties of care must be the same as those based on contract.

The same has to be true for liability based on *culpa in contrahendo* (negligence prior to conclusion of contract, *cf.* Case 11).[10]

It seems that liability for the statements in a prospectus has to be judged differently because conclusion of a contract is not intended by the person responsible for the prospectus and therefore *culpa in contrahendo* has to be ruled out. Nevertheless, it is generally accepted that the person who is responsible for the prospectus must compensate even pure economic loss caused negligently by incorrect statements. The explanation is that the person responsible for the prospectus evokes confidence by declaring his expert knowledge, he aims at influencing the investors, he knows that the investors are dependent on the prospectus and he is working for his own gain.[11]

More limited is liability based on '*Verträge mit Schutzwirkung zugunsten Dritter*' (contracts with protective purpose in favour of third parties). As a rule, under Austrian law pure economic interests of third parties are not included under the protective purpose.[12] The reason is, that each third party owns a separate property and, therefore, liability would be extended very far if their pure economic interests would be included in the protective purpose. Furthermore, it has to be considered that the tortfeasor does not pursue his interests towards the third party. But the duties to take care of the person of the third party and his rights of property are the same as between the parties of a contract.

If the parties take up contact without business interests, no duties to take care to pure economic interests are established. But other duties are still more intensive than under tort law, e.g., each partner has to take action to safeguard the partner and his property from harm.[13] Similar intensification of duties of care is established by '*Eröffnung des Verkehrs mit der Umwelt*' (opening of intercourse with the world around) and, perhaps, between adjacent owners.

If the opening of intercourse is in public interest, duties to maintain safety are almost not intensified. The duties to take action are restricted to warn about dangers.

The last link of the chain is the normal tortious liability which steps in if no special contact exists between the tortfeasor and the injured party.

---

10  *Cf.* Welser, *Vertretung ohne Vollmacht* (1970), p.73 ff.
11  *Cf.* Canaris, *Larenz-FS* (1983), p. 92 f., 94.
12  *Cf.* OGH in SZ 61/64; JBl 1990, 801; ÖBA 1991, 525 with commentary by Canaris; Koziol, *Österreichisches Haftpflichtrecht* II (2nd ed. 1984), p.87 f.
13  *Cf.* Michalek, *Die Haftung des Bergsteigers bei alpinen Unfällen*, (Diss. Wien 1990), p. 97 ff.

# The Nature of the Interests Protected by Tort Law

## Helmut Koziol

One can say that all interests are protected by tort law as long as they are not illegal or against *bonos mores*. But the decisive and rather difficult question is to what level they are protected. There is quite a difference between, on the one hand, the far-reaching protection of the traditional absolute rights and, on the other hand, of pure economic interests or of pure immaterial interests. However, I have to stress that even pure economic interests are protected further if there is a special relationship or contact between the malefactor and the sufferer (*cf.* the paper on the borderline between contract and tort). Thus, the scope of protection of an interest does not only depend on its nature but also on the proximity between tortfeasor and endangered person.

Regarding the nature of interests, I already pointed out in my paper on 'unlawfulness' (I.C.2.) that the extent of protection of rights or interests depends on whether one or more of a number of factors are given, also in which intensity and in which combination with other factors. One can infer from the ABGB and other statutes, further from doctrine and court decisions that the following factors are relevant for the level of protection of an interest: the value of the interest, its clear contours, its obviousness and which interests of third parties are restricted by its protection.

The highest ranked rights are those of *personality* and among these the rights to life, to physical well-being and to liberty are at the top. These three rights have, furthermore, clear contours and they are obvious. As no higher ranked rights of third parties are restricted by their protection, they enjoy, therefore, the most complete protection.

Other rights of personality do not have such clear contours, e.g., the right to privacy and the general right of personality which is accepted by some scholars. On the other hand, the protection of some rights of personality is apt to restrict rights of high rank of third parties. For example, the extensive protection of the right to honour and reputation comes inevitably into conflict with the right of others to free statement of opinion and with the public interest to know about criminal conduct or behaviour *contra bonos mores* of persons in public positions. Therefore, one has to look for a borderline of the protected sphere which does not restrict unreasonably the rights of others.

The *rights in rem* are due to high rank, they have clear contours and they are obvious. Therefore, they also enjoy very far-reaching protection. But, of course, unlimited protection would unreasonably restrict similar rights *in rem* of other persons, e.g., the right of the neighbours to use their property. Thus it is inevitable to restrict the protection

*H. Koziol (ed.), Unification of Tort Law: Wrongfulness, 29–30.*

of property for the sake of the neighbours. In this spirit, § 364 sec 2 ABGB rules that every landowner has to tolerate intromissions customary in the locality if they only impair the use of his property in a nonessential way. Finally, the protection of property is restricted also in the interest of the public (*cf.* § 364 sec 1 ABGB).

The *intangible property rights* rank as high as the rights in rem and they also have clear contours. Furthermore, they are either obvious as such, e.g., the author's right, or they can be made obvious by registration and enjoy protection only under this condition, e.g., patent rights and titles to a trade mark.

*Contractual rights* are, perhaps, lower ranking than the above mentioned interests and, what weighs even more, they are not obvious and their content varies. Furthermore, far-reaching protection of contractual rights would lead to an unreasonable restriction of freedom of movement of third parties. They had to be prepared to get liable if they did not make extensive inquiries. In the end, one has to consider that the interests of third parties will be of the same weight as those of the creditor. These are the reasons why interference with contractual relationships is judged as unlawful only if the tortfeasor was aware of the contract and acted with the intent to procure the debtor to breach of contract.

*Pure economic interests*, e.g., the chance to net a profit, are of lower rank than contractual rights as they did not yet take shape in a right and they are without clear content. Furthermore, they are not obvious and the interests of third parties are very often of the same or of a higher value. Therefore, third parties are allowed to cause pure economic loss even with intent, e.g., by fair competition or by seizing the opportunity to earn a profit. Under tort law, causing pure economic losses is unlawful only if the interests of the tortfeasor have to be valued much lower then those of the injured party or if the tortfeasor offends against good morals.

At the most to the same extent reaches the protection of pure immaterial interests. The reasons are the same and, in addition, it has to be considered that pure immaterial loss is unmeasurable. Therefore, the behaviour that causes fear, worry, unease[1] or disgust[2] regularly is not unlawful.[3] But an exception has to be made in case of intent to cause immaterial harm or of conduct *contra bonos mores*.

---

1    *Cf.* OGH in EvBl 1983/82.
2    *Cf.* OGH in EvBl 1983/82; JBl 1989, 41; SZ 61/109 = EvBl 1988/150.
3    In this sense already Bydlinski, 'Der Ersatz ideellen Schadens als sachliches und methodisches Problem', JBl 1965, 244.

# Belgium

## WRONGFULNESS IN BELGIAN TORT LAW

## Herman A. Cousy

I.   The legal basis of the Belgian law of tort is (still) to be found in Articles 1382 and 1383 of the (Napoleonic) Code Civil (hereafter called Civil Code), establishing the general principle of fault-liability, and in the subsequent Articles 1384 to 1386*bis* of the Civil Code, establishing special rules of ('presumed') or even faultless liability, attached to specific qualities of persons (owner, possessor of goods or of animals, parent, teacher or supervisor of persons).

It is traditionally and generally stated that according to the general rule laid down in Articles 1382/1383 of the Civil Code, liability depends upon the fulfilment of the three requirements: fault, damage and causation.

Whereas the concept unlawfulness plays a central role in the system of the German BGB and in the thereby inspired codifications[1], the concept of '*illicéite*' (*onrechtmatigheid*) has not succeeded in being substituted (or even added) to the concept of fault in systems like the Belgian one, which derive from French law. But doctrinal differences of view continue to exist with respect to the precise definition of what is fault and to the exact role that the concept of wrongfulness (or 'unlawfulness', '*onrechtmatigheid*') is playing within (as a part of) the more general concept of fault.

II.   According to what can be considered to be the (by now) classical view, the concept of fault consists of two elements: an objective and a subjective one. Contrary to what the concept suggests, the subjective element does not refer to any actual culpability. The subjective element has in fact boiled down to the sole requirement that the defendant must not be in such a situation that his act cannot be imputed to him. This is the case for children, mentally ill persons and for those who lose control of their acts. According to some authors, 'imputability' is also taken away by the existence of 'justification grounds'.[2]

The objective element is the unlawful behaviour. According to what would seem to be the majority view (and what is here called the classical view) a further distinction

---

1   J. Limpens, 'La faute et l'acte illicéite en droit comparé', *Melanges Dabin* II (1963), Brussel, Bruylant, pp. 723-741.
2   L. Cornelis, *Principes du droit belge de la responsabilité extracontractuelle* (1990), Bruylant, No. 18.

*H. Koziol (ed.), Unification of Tort Law: Wrongfulness*, 31–38.

must here be made between two types of such unlawful behaviour. One type consists in the violation of a specific and mandatory legal rule: such a violation is unlawful by itself (one could speak here of 'illegal' behaviour). A second type of unlawful behaviour is the violation of the general rule of behaviour, i.e. the general duty of care. We are dealing here with what is sometimes called an 'open norm', i.e. a norm the exact contents of which must be filled in by the judge on basis of the 'reasonable man' or *'bonus pater familias'* test. According to the very widely known formula, the question must be raised whether a normally prudent and reasonable man (human being), placed in the same factual circumstances would have acted differently. Among the elements to be taken into account in carrying out this evaluation are the foreseeability of the damage and the avoidability of the harm. The factual circumstances which must be taken into account are solely the external circumstances (like time, place, climate, social status, education, and professional ability) and not the purely subjective or internal circumstances such as the individual qualities of the defendant. There is no need to underline that the dividing line between objective/external and subjective/internal remains delicate. It should be underlined that the reference to the 'normally prudent and reasonable person' is meant to be a 'normative' criterion (what can be expected from such a person) and not simply a reference to what is *'de facto'* usual.[3]

One will notice that according to the here above described theory or view, the mere violation of a specific legal duty or rule implies unlawfulness, whereas in the case of the violation of a general rule of careful behaviour, additional requirements (such as the foreseeability and avoidability of harm, and more generally the evaluation of the *'bonus pater familias'* behaviour) must be fulfilled. Support for this view is found in a much discussed decision of the Cour de Cassation of 22 September 1988.[4]

As to the question whether the violation of a specific subjective right (like the right of property, the rights relating to the protection of the 'personality') constitutes in itself a fault in the sense of the Articles 1382/83 of the Civil Code, the answer is given that this situation is comparable to that of the violation of a specific legal rule or obligation.[5] It would nevertheless appear that in order to consider a violation of such a right (like e.g., the freedom of expression) as a fault a careful weighing of competing interests is necessary: the mere violation of another's right thus appears to not always be *per se* unlawful.

---

3   Vansweevelt, *De civielrechtelijke aansprakelijkheid van de geneesheer in het ziekenhuis* (1992), Maklu-Bruylant, No. 161, p. 149.

4   Cass., 22 September 1988, Pas., 1989, 1, 83. It was held that 'sous reserve de l'existence d'une erreur invincible ou d'un autre cause d'exonération de responsabilité (...), la transgression d'une norme légale est constitutive de faute' (Brussel, 28 April 1992, J.L.M.B., 1994, 40, decided upon referral by Cass. 22 September 1988; comp. Vandenberghe, van Quickenborne, Wynant, 'Overzicht van rechtspraak, aansprakelijkheid uit onrechtmatige daad 1985-1993', *Tijdschrift voor Privaatrecht* 1995, No. 3, 1115*).*

There is, however, another Cour de cassation decision of the same date which seems to give support to the opposing view (i.e., mere violation of a statutory duty does not equal fault): Cass., 22 September 1988, *Revue Critique de Jurisprudence Belge* 1990, 203, with observations by Dalcq, 'Appreciation de la faute en cas de violation d'une obligation determinée'.

5   Vandeberghe e.a., *l.c.,* No. 11, p. 1167.

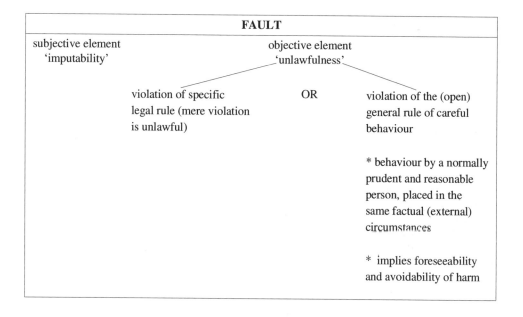

III. According to more recent doctrinal insights[6] the fault of Article 1382 Code Civil contains three elements: imputability of the acts to the tortfeasor, violation of a general rule of careful behaviour and the predictability of damage. The violation of a specific legal rule or of a subjective right does not constitute a separate subcategory of fault behaviour. For such violations, just as for the violation of the general rule of careful behaviour, the same test applies: the question must be asked whether a normally prudent and careful person would have behaved similarly while placed in the same factual circumstances. Justification grounds (such as situations of need, or of coercion, or order of public authorities, etc.) do constitute – in this approach – a factor of non-imputability rather than a factor of non-lawfulness.

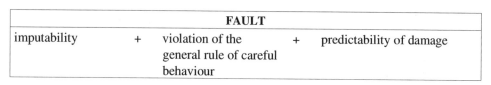

IV. It is generally accepted that Belgian law does not accept the theory of 'relative unlawfulness' ('*relatieve onrechtmatigheid*'), which is, e.g., found in the well-known German '*Schutznorm-Theorie*'). According to this theory a behaviour is only unlawful towards those whose interests are protected by the violated rule. The limitations which in other traditional legal systems derive from such a concept of 'relative' unlawfulness,

---

6    *See* mainly L. Cornelis, *Principes du droit belge de responsabilité extra-contractuelle, L'acte illicéite* (1990), Maklu-Bruylant, 779 pp.; L. Cornelis, *Beginselen van het Belgische buitencontractuele aansprakelijkheidsrecht, De onrechtmatige daad* (1989), Maklu-Bruylant, 744 pp.

will, under Belgian law, be handled as issues of causation: a perfect manner to complicate things. It may, however, very well be that while assessing causal relationships, considerations concerning the specific interests which are protected by a legal rule, are reintroduced through the back door.[7]

## V. The Cases

### A. Case 1

D's behaviour, consisting in opening a hairdresser salon next door to P, and in fiercely competing with P, and even consisting in driving him out of business, is perfectly lawful. There are, however, certain specific circumstances in which such behaviour can nevertheless become unlawful. There are limits to D's freedom to compete, the transgression of which makes D's behaviour unlawful.

A first possibility here is that the behaviour is characterised by '*abus de droit*'. In the absence of a contractual relationship, '*abus de droit*' falls within the scope of Articles 1382/1383 Code Civil. Among the clearly established subcategories of '*abus de droit*' are those where a person is exercising his right with the sole intention of causing harm to another person.[8] It would appear that the attitude of D can be so interpreted because of the specific antecedents and the subsequent closure of the competitive activity (although such attitude will be difficult to prove).

Another avenue is to examine the limits to D's right of competing with P consists in applying fair trade law. The question is whether 'ruthlessly undercutting prices with the (ultimate) purpose of driving the competitor out of business', constitutes an unfair trade practice. Suppose that one could establish that D was selling at a loss. Selling at a loss is not a specifically forbidden unfair practice (Article 40 of the 1991 Fair Trade Practices Act[9] concerning selling at a loss is only applicable to the sale of goods, and not to the 'sale of services'). But selling services at a loss can come under the general clause of Article 93 of the Fair Trade Practices Act which prohibits all acts which are contrary to fair trade practices (in French: *usages honnêtes du commerce*), by which a seller violates or can violate the professional interests of another seller. There is case law authority that states that ruthless competition which leads (and is intended to lead) to the destabilisation of the economic life of the competitor, does constitute such unfair practice, and is thus unlawful behaviour in the sense of Article 1382 Code Civil. Authors

---

7   In order to assess the existence of a causal relationship the question must be put whether the damage would take place if the unlawful act would not have taken place. It is thus required that the unlawfulness is essential, rather than a mere aspect of the unlawful deed. In order to assess this aspect of unlawfulness, arguments about the purpose of the violated rule may very well re-enter the play. *Cf.* J. Ronse, *Aanspraak op schadeloosstelling uit onrechtmatige daad* (1954), Brussel, Bruylant, No. 89, p.87.

8   Cass., 10 September 1971, *Arr. Cass.*, 1972, 31.

9   Fair Trade Practices Act (Wet van 14 juli 1991 betreffende de handelspraktijken en de voorlichting en bescherming van de consument, B.S., 29 augustus 1991, err., B.S., 10 oktober 1991).

also underline that the unlawfulness must be appreciated by reference to the interest of the consumer.[10]

## B. Case 2

This triangle situation presents a case of unfair competition falling under Article 93 of the Fair Trade Practices Act. More specifically the situation is one of complicity in the breach of contract by a contracting party. The question arises whether D is behaving unlawfully toward P by hiring X, while X was under the obligation solely to perform for P.

After having hesitated in its early decisions on the subject matter,[11] the Cour de Cassation has by now clearly established its doctrine that a third party is acting unlawfully and incurs liability towards a contracting party while knowingly participating in the breach of contract committed by the other contracting party. The present case does perfectly fit into these conditions.

It is by contracting with X that D is indeed participating in the very act by which X is violating her own contractual obligations towards P. In such circumstances the only further requirement is that D does contract with X knowingly, i.e., knowing that X is breaching her contractual obligations towards P.[12]

## C. Case 3

The question is whether the mere fact that Y is violating a statutory obligation or duty, in the course of his competitive action toward X, constitutes a wrongful act. It is well understood that Y is undoubtedly acting unlawfully but the violated obligation (of not stopping at red traffic lights) really has nothing to do with the organisation of the competition between X and Y to reach A first.

It should again be emphasised that Belgian law has no concept of relative unlawfulness. Therefore X's claim against Y could not be rejected because of the fact that traffic regulations were not intended to protect Y in the competition to reach A.

This situation is comparable to the one where two delivery services both try to reach a distant consumer first and where one of the two competitors wins the race by virtue of systematically ignoring traffic lights. Here the question arises whether such activity falls under the general rule of Article 93 of the Fair Trade Practices Act of 14 July 1991. It is clearly established theory that illegal behaviour (*onrechtmatig gedrag*) does in principle constitute unlawful behaviour (*onrechtmatig gedrag*) and that an '*action en cessation*' can be brought against such illegal (and thus unlawful) attitude. However, this possibility to bring an '*action en cessation*' does not necessarily guarantee a successful action in damages on the basis of Art. 1382 Code Civil. In order for an action in damages to be successful, not only does a fault need to be proven, but also a causal

---

10   G. Straetmans, 'Abusus non tollit usum', in: *Annuaire des pratiques du commerce* (1994), p. 297.
11   *See* Cass., 24 November 1932, Pas., 1933, I, 19.
12   *See* Cass., 22 April 1983, Arr. Cass., 1983, 1022 1028.

relationship between this fault and a proven damage (whereas an '*action de cessation*' can be brought on the basis of *possible* harm to the professional interests of the victim).

Case 3, however, presents the particularity of dealing with a competitive relationship outside the professional sphere, but as such does not alter the rules of causality. The question is here whether there exists a causal relationship between the traffic violation and the untimely reaching of A. In my view no such causal relationship exists.

## D. Case 4

Case 4 resembles Case 3 in the sense that here again the question arises as to whether the violation of a specific statutory obligation by one of the two competitors constitutes unlawful behaviour leading to liability in tort of the winner against the loser. The difference lies in the number of intervening factors between the law-breaking act and the damage. It is not the unlawful oil delivery by D which prevents P from pursuing his business. The oil delivery by D causes a prolongation of the civil war and this in turn prevents P from resuming his (lawful) oil delivery to Ruritania. The causality issue thus becomes (still) more delicate.

## E. Case 5

Does a normally prudent and reasonable man give dishonest and incorrect information to induce public authority to a certain action? I should think that the answer is no and that under Belgian law, D's attitude would be considered to violate the general duty of care to be expected from participants in a take-over battle. The question of whether an action in tort will lie, depends here more upon the question of whether the loss of a chance by P constitutes a damage (which it does) and whether there is a causal relationship between the misrepresentation and the damage (which the terms of the question seem to confirm).

## F. Case 6

As has been indicated above, there is some unclearness about the question of whether the mere violation of subjective rights, more particularly the infringement of a 'personality right', is in itself wrongful. The prudent answer is that this violation has to be caused by a fault, and that the appreciation thereof depends upon a delicate balancing of conflicting rights and interests. In this case at least two fundamental rights are at stake: the freedom of speech (Art. 10 European Convention Human Rights – E.C.H.R.) and the right to privacy (Art. 8 E.C.H.R.). The judge must weigh the interests at stake. Taking Art. 8, 1 E.C.H.R. concerning the protection of private life into account, one may state that publication in a newspaper must be in accordance with the truth, must not be needlessly aggrieving and must respect one's privacy.[13] Public interest is also at stake: the customers of that bank have a right to know the risk.

---

13   Cass., 13 September 1991, Arr.Cass., 1991-92, 46.

Note that Belgian Legislation on Credit Institutions (Act of 22 March 1993, made pursuant to E.C. directives) would make it impossible for A to exercise the function of director of a private bank after having been condemned for financial fraud.

## G. Case 7

While Case 6 deals with the (possible) violation of the right to privacy, Case 7 appears to concern a situation where the victim suffers injury, not to one of his (fundamental) rights, but where he has possibly suffered damage because of the violation of a legitimate interest, namely his interest in an accurate interpretation of his attitude. It makes no great difference whether we deal with the first situation or with the second (violation of a right or of a legitimate interest) since neither in the case of violation of the right nor in the case of the violation of a legitimate interest of P, an action in tort can be deduced from the mere fact of such violation or damage. In both cases the additional requirement must be satisfied that D has not acted as a *bonus pater familias* would have done, thus that D must have acted in breach of his duty to take reasonable care. Such violation implies that the damage to P must be foreseeable and avoidable. In the appreciation of the duty of care, delicate balancing of interests will have to take place. While expressing a judgement upon the quality of his former employee, D must be able to express himself freely, and to even express his personal disappointment or malcontentment with P. Such is in the best interest of X, and ultimately of P. D must thus be entrusted with a certain 'margin' of appreciation, and can only be considered to act wrongfully if his judgement is such as to transgress the said margin, i.e. if no reasonable man would have acted like D under the circumstances.

## H. Case 8

This appears to be a case in which the question arises if and to what extent a possible self-defence can take away the wrongfulness of the act. The concept of self-defence is well known as a concept of penal law. The Belgian Cour de Cassation as yet has not had the occasion to clarify its contents and limits in the context of civil liability.

Perhaps there is also a question whether the restaurant owner had been induced into error, in such a way as to justify his damage inflicting behaviour. Error, however, must be invincible to serve as a justification ground and it is doubtful whether the restaurateur's error as to the payment was invincible.

Both self-defence and error are 'justification grounds' which take away the faulty character.

## I. Case 9

According to Belgian law, conditions of liability do not depend upon the nature of damage: the damage can be of a physical nature, or of a pecuniary or of a purely 'moral' nature. Every such damage must be compensated if it is caused by a fault of the tortfeasor.

To answer the question whether physical or economic harm or nuisance give rise to an action for damages, the same conditions of liability apply.

It should be noted that with respect to nuisance a judicially made doctrine of 'liability without fault' has emerged. This theory (called the equilibrium theory), based not on Article 1382 C.C. but on Article 544 C.C. (definition of the right of property) holds that the owner of a piece of real estate who even by rightful use of his property causes exceptional nuisance to his neighbours, is obliged to pay them reasonable compensation. Exercising an industrial activity without a legally required permit is wrongful. The resulting damages (of whatever nature) will be recoverable in tort.

Exercising an activity under the protection of the required authorization or permit does not confer immunity against tort liability. Indeed holding a legally required authorization is a necessary, but not a sufficient condition for non-liability.

In the same vein, firmly established case law confirms that the fulfilment of precise and regulatory duties is generally not sufficient to protect a person against all possible civil liability. An act which is not violating any particular legal prescription, may still be faulty, if it is committed in violation of the general duty of care.

## J. Case 10

(a) Ever since 1961 there has been Article 422*bis* of the Penal Code which imposes penal sanctions upon a person who omits to render help to a person in serious danger, while being able to do so without serious threat of danger to himself or to others. A violation of this penal obligation leads to civil liability.

Article 422*bis* of the Penal Code specifies that the obligation of help rests upon the person who has himself observed the dangerous situation as well as upon any person to whom the danger was described by those calling for his help.

It is clear that not only in situation c (where the doctor is probably under a professional ethical duty to give help) but also in hypothesis a, D would be penally and civilly liable.

(b) Hypothesis b deals with the creation of a dangerous situation. Under Belgian law, the creation of a dangerous situation does not constitute in itself a fault. Such is the case only if the danger is created without necessity or if the author has negligently omitted to take the measures necessary to avoid danger to others.

# England

WRONGFULNESS UNDER ENGLISH TORT LAW

## W. V. Horton Rogers

## I. General

In one sense 'wrongfulness' plays a major part in English tort law, indeed is at the foundation of it. The law of torts is, after all, the law of 'civil wrongs'. But from another point of view the concept is almost meaningless since 'wrong'/'wrongfulness' may be regarded as merely a shorthand description of the situations in which tort liability is imposed. On this basis the statement that 'torts are wrongful acts' is not very helpful since, unless we recount all the rules of tort law, it does not tell us anything about the ingredients which constitute wrongfulness. In any event, it is also an over extensive description because, for example, breaches of contract or of trust are to us also 'wrongful' in the sense that they give rise to private rights of action the outcome of which may be not dissimilar to a claim in tort[1] – generally the payment of financial compensation by the defendant to the plaintiff.[2] You own a painting. I steal it. I commit the tort of conversion which requires me to pay you its value. I am trustee of a fund of money which I hold for your benefit and I misappropriate it. I am liable on the basis of breach of trust to make good that deficiency. I doubt if the layman would see much difference between the two cases and the fact that my liability rests upon a different basis stems from the fact that, historically, you were not the legal 'owner' of the fund (nor were you in possession of it) but the Court of Chancery treated you as if you were, though it fashioned its own remedies rather than using those of the common law courts. That is why, even though there is no real practical day to day difficulty in recognizing tort's

---

1   Sir Percy Winfield's famous definition emphasized that tort liability was imposed by law and applied to persons generally whereas contractual liability arose by consent. Even aside from the fact that it is the law which decides to make contracts enforceable, there are many difficulties in this approach, in particular that many contractual duties arise from implied terms which are virtually or even wholly independent of the will of the parties and that tort liability may arise to an individual or to a limited group of persons on the basis of 'undertaking'.

2   It is harder to say that restitutionary liability is founded on 'wrong'. Sometimes it is. If I steal your picture and sell it for more than its market value you have a restitutionary claim against me for the price I obtained but the liability is based upon my tort in having taken it. But if I innocently receive from you a mistaken overpayment on our accounts it seems difficult to say that this is a 'wrong'.

*H. Koziol (ed.), Unification of Tort Law: Wrongfulness*, 39–55.

territory, a definition seeking technical accuracy tends to end up with something very unhelpful like 'a tort is a claim based upon a situation which before the Common Law Procedure Act 1852 would have been remediable by an action of trespass or an action on the case or is analogous to such a situation,[3] or which is classified as tort by statute'.[4] There is also the well-known negative approach, 'A tort is a civil wrong other than a breach of contract or a breach of trust' which, as Wigmore (I think it was) once said, is rather like defining chemistry by saying it is not physics and it is not mathematics.

Perhaps I worry too much about the problem of assigning liability among the categories and that our broad use of 'wrong' is simply a matter of terminology. To take a more positive approach, let us assume that the broad ideas of contract, tort, trust etc. are clear enough. Can we then arrive at some concept of 'wrongfulness' which will enable us to say, 'Yes, this form of liability belongs in the tort section of the code because it has this characteristic'?

At the very highest level of abstraction a broad idea of wrongfulness is reconcilable with the common law, if only because there are clearly situations – as there must be in every system – where damage caused is not actionable, even leaving aside defences in the proper sense.[5] Any tort law must contain (or imply) some rules of non-liability. Even expressions found in the NBW like 'pertaining to proper social conduct' or matters for which the defendant is answerable 'according to common opinion' can be matched by judicial statements of a similarly vague nature about the law reflecting the demands of society (as perceived by the courts) for reasonable protection from the damage causing activities of others.[6] At the end of what is probably the best short account of the nature and role of tort law, Dean Prosser said: 'So far as there is one central idea, it would seem that it is that liability must be based upon conduct which is socially unreasonable. The common thread woven into all torts is the idea of unreasonable interference with the interests of others.'[7] The practical difficulty – and a common lawyer cannot help thinking in this way – is that no one would think of *enacting* such a broad principle because it is very much an ultimate source of last resort for the final appellate court. Most novel cases are decided not by reference to such broad principles but by reference to existing case law[8] and where it is wished to expand the law the tendency is to do it gradually by increment. I will not repeat what I have said

---

3    This is necessary to allow for the fact that the courts have undoubtedly created new forms of liability since the abolition of the forms of action.
4    The last part leads to some strange inclusions. Technically, the whole of liability for discrimination on the grounds of race, sex or disability and liability for breach of copyright and patents is 'tort' but one would never see more than the most cursory reference to these matters in a 'tort book.'
5    On the difficulty caused by excluding defences *see* below, I.
6    Indeed, a good case can be made for saying that English (and other common law) courts are more explicit about 'matters of policy' than continental courts. For an extreme example, though in a highly technical area, *see Marc Rich AG* v. *Bishop Rock Marine Co.* [1995] 3 WLR 227.
7    Prosser & Keeton, *Torts* (5th ed. 1984), p. 6.
8    Of course there are statutes, indeed Christian von Bar (*A Common European Law of Torts* (1996), Centro di studi e ricerche di diritto comparato e straniero, Roma) says that England has the greatest number of specific statutes on torts of any European country. But these are 'islands' in a sea of case law and the most important of them deal either with 'ancillary matters' such as limitation (prescription) and the effect of death or they are detailed amendments of parts of an area rooted in the common law (e.g., the Defamation Act 1996).

before in a Tilburg context about the 'duty of care' but I think it may be instructive to quote what was our first major attempt to reduce this to a broad formula:

'The rule that you are to love your neighbour becomes in law: You must not injure your neighbour, and the lawyer's question: Who is my neighbour? receives the restricted reply. You must take reasonable care to avoid acts or omissions which you can reasonably foresee would be likely to injure your neighbour. Who then in law is my neighbour? The answer seems to be persons who are so closely and directly affected by my act that I ought reasonably to have them in contemplation as being so affected when I am directing my mind to the acts or omissions which are called in question.'[9]

Now the actual issue in this case was whether a negligent manufacturer of dangerous goods could be liable to the ultimate user with whom he had no contractual relationship and the answer 'Yes' is now regarded as self-evidently correct.[10] But the attempt to use this formula as a general and sufficient test of the existence of liability for negligence has resulted in an enormous quantity of litigation and used for this purpose today it would be seriously misleading, because it fails to take account of whole areas where liability based on 'foreseeability' is excluded or at least restricted. Again, it is a matter of the level of abstraction at which the statement is made. 'It is wrongful (i.e., actionable) to cause harm by negligence' would serve if your purpose was to provide a citizen with a general idea of tort law, though it would be seriously misleading for someone who proposed to take action on the basis of it. Hence, while negligence is an ingredient (among other forms of conduct) in a wrongful act it is not in itself a sufficient indicator of such an act. 'It is wrongful to cause physical damage by negligence' would be a workable rule of thumb for a general lawyer, though it is subject to certain exceptions. But the only accurate statement would be 'Negligence causing harm is wrongful where there has been a breach of a duty of care recognized by law in situations of that type (this duty being a complex based upon fairness, reasonableness, "justice" and the nature of the interest in respect of which protection is claimed)'. In other words, we come back to the problem of having to recount all the rules.

Nor is intentional conduct any more trustworthy an identifier of wrongfulness. Again the nature of the interest sought to be protected and the conduct sought to be sanctioned come into play. Intentional physical interference[11] with the body or property of another will amount to one of the trespass torts – assault, battery, false imprisonment etc.[12] This, however, raises a further difficulty. We have, for practical reasons, excluded

---

9   Lord Atkin in *Donoghue* v. *Stevenson* [1932] AC 562.

10  The principle is of little practical importance in relation to consumers since the Consumer Protection Act 1987, but it is still the governing rule in relation to business users.

11  I have used this word rather than 'damage' since this, in its ordinary sense of physical trauma, is unnecessary – the trespass torts are actionable *per se*. If there is damage in the sense of physical trauma there is of course liability for it.

12  There is room for the view that we might simplify this area by running existing torts together. There is hardly any difference between assault and battery (the former is usually the inception

matters of justification or excuse from our examination of wrongfulness but the exclu-
sion causes difficulties in this area. If a police officer arrests me on reasonable suspicion
of an arrestable offence that it is not a tort but the burden of showing reasonable grounds
for suspicion lies upon him. In other words, from the point of view of pleading and proof
the common law takes as its starting point that unconsented[13] to interference is a tort (or,
if you prefer, is wrongful). Yet looking at the position as a whole, I think the instinct of
the common lawyer would be to say that the lawfulness of the arrest made the
interference 'not wrongful'.[14] If we move outside the simple trespass torts then the
proposition that intentional harm is wrongful is even harder to maintain. I compete with
you using only means which do not contravene the law. That is not a tort. Nor can you
throw on me the burden of showing that my conduct was lawful. Rather, it is up to you
to establish some basis for an allegation of one of the 'economic' torts such as conspiracy
or interference with contract. So one cannot even say it is *prima facie* wrongful. The
best one can say is that it is 'commonly' wrongful.

There remain cases of strict liability. Where a system of law imposes liability upon
D simply because D's conduct or activity has caused harm to P it seems a curious use
of language to say that D has committed a 'wrong' against P.[15] However, at common
law there is always some requirement of liability, even if not 'fault' in the general sense,

---

[Note 12 continued]
of or the threat of the latter). False imprisonment of course deals with rather a different factual
situation. A ripe candidate for revision is the requirement that in the trespass torts the act must be
'direct'. This requires us to say that if D hits P that is battery, whereas if D poisons P that is a
different tort, an 'action on the case' commonly known by the name of the leading case *Wilkinson*
v. *Downton* [1897] 2 QB 57. The directness requirement disappeared in the United States. That
this did not happen here may owe something to the fact that in the middle of the 19th century we
abolished the 'forms of action' i.e., we removed the procedural consequences of having different torts.

13    The cases indicate that the absence of consent is part of the plaintiff's case, i.e. it is not a justification
or excuse *stricto sensu*. While this may be true in terms of pleading it probably does not have
much practical significance – if P denies that he consented to the contact a practical burden is
likely to fall on D to show that he did.

14    This problem (which perhaps does no more than demonstrate the unsystematic nature of the
common law) is even more obvious in the case of defamation. A workable practical definition of
defamation would be 'a false statement liable to damage the plaintiff's reputation'. Yet, in the
English common law it is not incumbent upon the plaintiff to prove falsity, it is for the defendant
to prove truth. Why do we not then bring other defences into the basic definition ('defamation is
a false statement liable to damage the plaintiff's reputation and which is not made on an occasion
of privilege or as a fair comment on a matter of public interest')? In fact, the position is even more
complicated. If the defendant shows that the words were used on an occasion of qualified privilege
the plaintiff may still rebut that defence by showing that they were used with malice.

15    Though it could be said that this was in a sense the position of the early common law in respect
of direct physical interference with the person. Trespass to the person simply required P to show
that D had made 'direct' physical contact with him. Liability was not truly strict but it was incumbent
on D to show an excuse – e.g., inevitable accident (similar to lack of negligence in modern
terminology). This is not the present law. P has to show intention or negligence.

which goes beyond a mere causal relationship between the defendant's activity and the plaintiff's injury.[16]

## II. The Cases

### A. Cases 1 to 5: Introduction

This group of cases covers what are loosely called the 'economic torts.' It would be idle to pretend that these present a wholly logical structure but the prominence of the idea of 'unlawful means' in this area bears some resemblance (though a superficial and misleading one) to an underlying common theme of 'wrongfulness.' Because the material is complex it is probably best to begin with a short general introduction, with the warnings that some of what follows is necessarily a simplification which glosses over some controversial points. It may help to see these things 'graphically' and I have therefore included a very simplified chart of the basic heads of liability.

I. Conspiracy to injure

Def                                   Plf
(A & A2) _____ C
                        predominant intent to injure

II. Unlawful means conspiracy

(A & A2) _____ C
                    unlawful means + intent to injure

III. Directly inducing/procuring breach of contract

A _____ B _____ C
        persuasion                contract

IV. Directly procuring breach of contract by unlawful means

A _____ B _____ C
    unlawful means (e.g. tort)           contract

---

16   Whether this is so by statute of course depends on the terms of the statute. It is a question how far specific statutory liabilities should be incorporated in a general code. Thus the régime of traffic liability is not part of the CC but the régime under the Product Liability Directive is incorporated in the NBW.

## V. Indirectly procuring breach of contract by unlawful means

| A | X | B | C |
|---|---|---|---|
| persuasion | contract (e.g. employment) | contract (e.g. commercial contract) | |

## VI. Three party intimidation

| A | B | C |
|---|---|---|
| threat of unlawful act | contract or other expectation | |

## VII. Two party intimidation

| A | C |
|---|---|
| threat of unlawful act | |

## VIII. Interference with trade by unlawful means

| A | B | C |
|---|---|---|
| unlawful means | contract or other expectation | |

It is now generally accepted that there is a 'genus' tort of unlawful interference with trade or business by unlawful means (Tort VIII). This view has only prevailed in the last 20 years or so, the majority of the longer established economic torts being regarded as species of the genus (Torts II and IV to VII). Both the genus and the species are torts of intention in the sense that negligent interference with economic interests is actionable on a much more restricted basis. However, it is not wholly clear what 'intention' means. In the case of Tort I (which is outside the genus) there must clearly be a predominant intent to injure the plaintiff. This is not so in the other cases but there are at least two contending possibilities for the mental element in these cases: (a) the state of mind in which the acts of the defendant, although primarily intended to advance his own interests, are nevertheless 'aimed at' the plaintiff; (b) the state of mind in which the defendant is simply aware that his acts will have the effect of injuring the plaintiff. To take a simple example, A, a singer, contracts to make an album for B. As A knows, B engages C to provide the musical backing. A receives a better offer from elsewhere and breaks his contract with B. As A knows, this will have the effect of causing B to terminate his contract with C. Under approach (a) A commits no tort against C, who is a mere ricochet victim. Under approach (b) A may be liable in tort to C. A further complication, for which there is some support in the cases, is that the meaning of intention may differ from one tort to another (though this is difficult to reconcile with the species/genus metaphor).

The genus and the species torts have the further common characteristic that they require 'unlawful means,' that is to say some independently wrongful act (though not necessarily one directly actionable by the plaintiff). Unfortunately, there is a good deal of uncertainty as to what qualifies as unlawful means and whether that concept is the same under all headings. It can safely be said that a tort is unlawful means and that a breach of contract is, too. Paradoxical as it may seem, it is by no means clear that a crime is unlawful means (indeed, in the case of statutory crimes it is probably generally not). A cartel agreement which is void as in restraint of trade is not unlawful means.[17] However, not all of the cases are easily reconcilable and there appears to be a constant contest between those who wish to restrict liability by giving a narrow meaning to unlawful means and those who would extend it to 'any act which the defendant is not at liberty to commit.'[18] Certainly if we take the broad view of unlawful means we are in danger of ending up with the result that a haulage company which infringes the rules on drivers' hours or a restaurant which cuts corners on hygiene may not only be prosecuted by the relevant authority but also sued by rivals who lose business because they cannot match the infringers' prices.

One reason for the considerable degree of uncertainty on these issues is that most modern cases have been decided on applications by defendants to strike out or by plaintiffs for interlocutory injunctions, where the issue is whether the claim is arguable and the court does not have to make a definitive decision at that stage. A tactical victory by the plaintiff at this stage often leads to an out of court settlement, leaving the fundamental issue tantalizingly uncertain.

Torts IV and V are necessarily confined to the case where there is an interference with an existing contract, though the shorthand expression 'breach of contract' is sometimes too narrow: for example, in Tort IV if A kidnaps B to prevent B performing his contract with C, A plainly commits a tort against C, even though B, if sued for breach of contract by C, might have the defence of impossibility. Torts VI and VIII, however, clearly extend beyond existing contracts – one of the earliest cases involved A threatening and using force against B to stop B coming to trade with C. Tort VII is of limited importance because unlawful threats by A directly to C will generally invalidate the resulting transaction between A and C and/or give C a restitutionary claim in respect of value transferred by C to A.

All this leaves Torts I and III. Tort III is arguably the 'core' economic tort. It requires no independently unlawful means: the mere persuasion is[19] actionable.[20] Some formulations bring this within the genus Tort VIII by saying that the persuasion itself is unlawful but this seems a mere matter of words. The case that cannot be brought within the genus tort is Tort I. This is unique (and some say anomalous) because it is the sole

---

17  *Mogul SS Co.* v. *McGregor Gow* [1892] AC 25.

18  Lord Denning MR in *Torquay Hotel Co.* v. *Cousins* [1969] 2 Ch 106 at 139.

19  Or, more accurately, may be actionable. There are of course cases in which A is justified in persuading B to break his contract with C, the most obvious being where B makes two inconsistent contracts with A and C and A, when he entered into his, was unaware of C's.

20  The reader may think that this tort and some of the others would render it impossible to call a strike in England. If it were the common law alone that would be so. However, since 1906 legislation has given immunity to action 'in contemplation or furtherance of a trade dispute'. This has been somewhat restricted since 1979 but the core element of immunity remains.

instance in English law of a bad motive making actionable an act which is not otherwise wrongful. However, it requires a combination – the 'magic of plurality.'

## B. Case 1

D's conduct is not tortious because there is no procurement of breach of an existing contract and no unlawful means are employed. Destroying a rival's business by predatory pricing to corner the market for yourself is not a legal wrong on the municipal law plane[21] and it does not become so because the sole purpose of the exercise is to ruin him.[22] The position would be different if D acted in combination with others[23] (Tort I) – though this is narrower than might be expected because for this purpose you cannot conspire with your employees. The tort is of very limited practical importance simply because it requires a predominant intention to injure the plaintiff. Therefore even the most ruthless pursuit of self-interest insulates the defendant from liability.[24] A few U.S states would impose liability on our facts without any element of combination.[25] Others would tend in the same direction on the theory of '*prima facie* tort', that is to say that once the plaintiff shows some intentional interference by the defendant liability follows unless the defendant can show some justification or privilege, e.g., competitive activity.[26]

## C. Case 2

These are the facts of *Lumley* v. *Gye*,[27] which established Tort III, procuring breach of contract by direct persuasion. At first it was associated with a much older liability based upon status – enticement of servants – but it cut loose entirely from that so that it is applicable to contracts generally. It forms a significant qualification to the doctrine of privity, whereby contracts only confer rights and impose duties between the parties thereto.

---

21  We may safely assume that this case does not attract Art 86 of the Treaty of Rome. Municipal competition law does not operate by way of actions for damages. It seems, however, that a contravention of Art 86 gives rise to an action for damages in English law: *Garden Cottage Foods* v. *Milk Marketing Board* [1984] AC 130.

22  *Mayor of Bradford* v. *Pickles* [1895] AC 587 (D, in revenge for P's refusal to buy his land, pumping away water which fed P's reservoir, but in which P had no proprietary right).

23  *See Crofter Hand Woven Harris Tweed Co.* v. *Veitch* [1942] AC 435.

24  So in the *Crofter* case the union's action, though ruinous to the plaintiffs, was not wrongful because its purpose was to raise the wages of the union members.

25  *Tuttle* v. *Buck* 119 NW 946 (Minn 1909) upon which this case is based.

26  Some English statements can be seen as supporting a similar approach, of which the best known is that of Bowen LJ in *Mogul SS Co.* v. *McGregor Gow* in the CA (1889) 23 Q.B.D. 598: 'Now, intentionally to do that which is calculated in the ordinary course of events to damage, and which does, in fact, damage another in that other person's property or trade, is actionable if done without just cause or excuse.'

27  (1853) 2 E & B 216.

## D. Case 3

Cases 3 and 4 may be taken together. In Case 3 if X sues Y for breach of statutory duty he would plainly fail. To establish liability for breach of a statute which does not expressly confer a civil right of action the plaintiff has to show two things: (a) that by implication the intention of the legislator was to confer a private right of action and (b) that the damage of which he complains is of a type against which the statute was designed to offer protection. X would fail on (a) because the clear trend is not to regard legislation of this type as giving rise to a civil action. Of course running the red light would be excellent evidence of negligence in the event of an accident but that is a different thing and of no relevance here. In any event, X would also fail on (b): the purpose of traffic light regulations is not to ensure fair behaviour in bidding for contracts.

At first sight it might appear that X could rely on Tort VIII. Y has used unlawful means with the purpose and effect of harming X's business.[28] However, it is virtually certain that this is not so for reasons that we now turn to in connection with Case 4.

## E. Case 4

*Case 4* is based on *Lonrho* v. *Shell Petroleum (No 2)*.[29] No attempt was made here to contend that the economic sanctions legislation gave rise to an action for breach of statutory duty but a claim was based on Tort VIII. This was rejected on the ground that if the legislation did not create a private right of action neither could its breach constitute unlawful means for Tort VIII. Shell were also alleged to have conspired with other oil companies and thereby to have committed Tort II. This claim also failed on the basis, it was thought, that the mental element required for Tort II was the same as that for Tort I, a predominant intention to injure, and this was clearly absent – Shell was out to increase its business and harming Lonrho was merely a side effect. We now know that this is an incorrect interpretation of the case and the mental element of Tort II is wider than that of Tort I.[30] Unfortunately, there was no discussion in *Lonrho* v. *Shell* of the meaning of unlawful means for the purposes of Tort II, but the better view is that here, too, contravention of a purely penal statute does not amount to unlawful means.

## F. Case 5

Case 5 is similar to *Lonrho* v. *Fayed*.[31] The conspiracy claim (Tort II) went to the House of Lords but the claim for Tort VIII went no further than the Court of Appeal, which declined to strike it out – in other words held that the pleaded facts disclosed an arguable

---

28  I put on one side the difficulties of proof that might arise over whether X would have got there first absent Y's crime.
29  [1982] AC 173. Note that the case was decided on an issue of law referred by an arbitrator and it was never proved that the defendants had done what was alleged.
30  *Lonrho* v. *Fayed* [1992] 1 AC 448. The fact that the plaintiff in the two cases is the same is coincidence.
31  [1992] 1 AC 448.

claim.[32] Two points are noteworthy. First, the unlawful means were the lies told by the defendants about themselves to the minister. Now lies intended to get another person to act to his detriment certainly amount to a tort (deceit or fraud) but on the facts it is hard to see how the target of the lies – the minister – had suffered any damage by being deceived, the damage was suffered by the rival bidder. In other words the unlawful means used were an incomplete tort against a third party. Secondly, some doubt was expressed whether interference with something so tenuous as the opportunity to bid could be described as interference with the plaintiff's trade. However, while Tort VIII has no doubt acquired its name because interference with trade is its normal setting, it is difficult to see any reason why it should be confined to trade (or business).[33]

## G. Case 6

False imputations upon a person's reputation are wrongful as defamation but there is no equivalent general protection of privacy. Certainly some forms of liability have the *effect* of protecting privacy (for example, trespass to land, breach of confidence, the provisions of the Data Protection Act 1984) but there is no unifying principle. The statement is defamatory (i.e., lowers the plaintiff in the estimation of respectable people) but truth[34] is a defence.[35] The sole qualification to this is the Rehabilitation of Offenders Act 1974, under which a conviction may become 'spent' after a period of time. If a plaintiff sues in respect of a statement imputing to him an offence for which the conviction is spent the defendant is not wholly deprived of the defence of truth but he loses it if the plaintiff can show that the publication was made with malice – i.e., spitefully or for an improper purpose. However, the Act is inapplicable to cases where the sentence was more than 30 months, which seems likely to be the case here.[36]

The absence of any specific legally protected right of privacy[37] is a frequent feature of common law systems – for example the general position is the same in Australia[38]

---

32 The action was never tried because the long running battle between Lonrho and the Fayed brothers over the control of Harrods was settled out of court.

33 Consider the following case. B contracts to buy C's house. A, wishing to obtain the house himself at a lower price, threatens B with violence if he goes ahead and B pulls out. A has committed Tort VI against C. If Tort VIII is the genus which includes the species, how can it be narrower in its scope?

34 The technical expression is justification but this does not mean that it must be in the public interest that the statement should be made.

35 A defence in the proper sense, i.e., it is up to the defendant to prove truth, not up to the plaintiff to prove falsity.

36 Even if the conviction was spent it is by no means obvious that the plaintiff could show malice here – *see* the reason which has led him to resign.

37 Although the European Court of Human Rights has taken a non-literal approach to Arts 8(1) and (2) of the Convention so that there may be an obligation to take measures to secure respect for private life even by non-state bodies (*X and Y* v. *Netherlands* A 91 (1985)) this does not, as I understand it, entail an obligation to introduce a 'law of privacy.'

38 However, in New South Wales the defence of truth is only available in a defamation action if the publication was in the public interest. This is English law in respect of *criminal* libel but that is more or less obsolete.

and Canada.[39] The area has been controversial in recent times and there have been judicial statements to the effect that if Parliament does not act the courts may have to do so.[40] However, there are profound difficulties in delineating the scope of the area of legitimate public interest in the lives of 'public figures,' particularly politicians. The position is, of course, radically different in the USA, where there is a highly developed common law liability, one aspect of which is the unauthorized publication of 'private facts.' However, the First Amendment has been at least as influential in privacy as in libel and many claims fail on the basis that there is a legitimate public interest in knowing the truth.

## H. Case 7

In order to be defamatory a statement need not necessarily involve an imputation of misconduct: it is plainly defamatory to say of a woman that she has been raped or of a trader that he is insolvent as a result of misfortune beyond his control. Possibly this statement could be defamatory but I propose to assume that it is not. In any event, if D's assessment were made in error but in good faith it would be protected in defamation law by qualified privilege.[41] However, it has now been held that quite independently of the law of defamation a person who provides a reference may owe a duty of care in negligence to the subject of the reference: *Spring* v. *Guardian Assurance*.[42] This is an interesting development because it adds a wholly new strand to the law governing 'reputation.' The burden on the plaintiff is certainly greater than under the general rules of defamation because here he must prove (a) that the statement was untrue (or not a tenable opinion) and (b) that he has suffered damage as a result. The latter element in particular may present serious difficulties where the purpose of the reference is to choose a short-list of candidates from a wide field.[43] However, the decision certainly adds new terrors for referees since formerly it was assumed that you were completely protected if you were honest (and it was up to the plaintiff to prove that you were not). Furthermore, while the liability is in theory one for negligence, if the inaccuracy is over a factual matter such as time-keeping or examination results the duty of 'care' will in practical terms amount to an obligation to get it right.

---

39  But some provinces have local privacy statutes.
40  There are regulatory bodies for the print and broadcast media which do admit complaints about invasion of privacy but they have no power to award damages, merely to require the offender to publish their adjudication.
41  For similar reasons there can be no liability for what is commonly known as malicious falsehood.
42  [1995] 2 AC 296.
43  But sometimes references are only sought as a check after a candidate has been provisionally chosen. A university student who had a job offer withdrawn in this way was recently awarded £50,000 against her university for an inaccurate reference.

## I. Case 8

The action of the owner (D) raises issues about the oldest form of tort liability, trespass. Trespass to the person[44] is subdivided into the two forms of battery and assault.[45] A battery is the direct application of force to the body of the plaintiff without legal justification. An assault is a threatened battery (e.g., pointing a gun).[46] Both torts (which are also crimes) are actionable *per se* – i.e., damages may be awarded even if the plaintiff suffers no bodily injury or financial loss, though the damages are of course likely to be much higher if there is some harm. Both torts require intentional wrongdoing. For purely historical reasons an 'indirect' intentional injury (e.g., poisoning someone or causing a nervous breakdown by maliciously starting a false report that a relative has been killed) is not trespass but it is undoubtedly a tort[47] and the distinction is not likely to have practical consequences today. It may therefore be fairly said that the common law recognizes a general principle that unjustified wilful bodily injury (and probably injury to tangible property) is tortious.[48]

This case would be likely to turn on the defences available to D. A person may use reasonable force in self-defence or the prevention of crime. Not surprisingly, almost all the case law on mistake is in the context of criminal prosecutions for assault, where the law appears to be that the issue is to be judged on what the defendant honestly (even though unreasonably) believed to be the circumstances. Though it is to some extent speculative, the civil law probably is that only a reasonable mistaken belief excuses the defendant. If, therefore, a reasonable person might have interpreted V's action as an assault, D has a defence, bearing in mind that the slight push is not a disproportionate response. It is important to stress that in a civil action the burden of proof on this issue is on D,[49] though the previous behaviour of V and his partner may assist on this.

If for some reason D cannot make out the defence the question arises of the extent of his liability. Remoteness of damage (legal causation) is normally determined by the test of reasonable foreseeability but at least in some cases of intentional wrongdoing the law is more severe and the defendant is liable for any direct consequences of his act, even if unforeseeable. The facts here are not sufficiently explicit to be certain whether this would be an issue. Though historically dubious it is probably the law that the Law Reform (Contributory Negligence) Act 1945 can be used to reduce even compensatory damages in a case of battery if the plaintiff has provoked the situation.

---

44   *Cf.* trespass to land, trespass to goods. Though in lay language trespass now probably suggests trespass to land, the legal sense is broader, that of 'wrong', as in the Lord's Prayer, 'forgive us our trespasses as we forgive those that trespass against us'.
45   A third form, false imprisonment, is irrelevant here.
46   Even lawyers commonly use 'assault' to cover both battery and assault *stricto sensu*.
47   *Wilkinson* v. *Downton* [1897] 2 QB 57. It would be bizarre if conduct which was actionable if done negligently (e.g., the poisoning) were not actionable if done intentionally.
48   Trespass is of course wider in that it is actionable *per se*. It has elements of a 'dignitary' wrong.
49   This is not necessarily true of a criminal prosecution. However, in practice the position is blurred by the fact that even though the formal burden of proof is on the prosecution the defendant may face a practical or 'evidential' burden in coming forward with some evidence to support a claim of mistake.

## J. Case 9

The first point is that A, B and C would be likely to be most concerned about getting an injunction to restrain further emissions rather than damages. However, they have to make out a case of nuisance in the same way as if they were seeking damages (save that merely threatened damage may be restrained by injunction). A nuisance is an unreasonable interference with the plaintiff's enjoyment (use) of his land and it clearly extends to disturbance of domestic use by noise, smells etc. Rights here are essentially relative because each landowner has to put up with a certain amount of interference as the price of being able to inflict comparable interference on neighbours in carrying out his own activities. As it has been put it is the law of 'give and take.' The issue of reasonableness/unreasonableness is only superficially the same as in the tort of negligence. There we are concerned with whether the defendant's behaviour came up to the standard required by law. Here we are primarily concerned with the effect of the defendant's activity upon the plaintiff–does it pass beyond the level of interference permitted by law, bearing in mind that the defendant must have the opportunity to pursue his legitimate activities? Because rights are relative motive is important – a defendant may be allowed to make X decibels of noise in carrying out a legitimate activity but not allowed to make the same amount of noise with the purpose of inconveniencing neighbours. Without more information it is not therefore possible categorically to say whether A, B and C do or do not have a claim. Since the smell is described as 'severe, nasty' it seems unlikely that A's reaction is unduly sensitive or idiosyncratic, nor is B's.[50] In C's case it is not the diminution in value as such which is the basis of the claim[51] but the fact that the diminution in value is caused by the discomfort. Again, however, the grant of an injunction should cure the diminution in value. Though the grant of the injunction is 'discretionary' and there is power to award damages in lieu, English courts tend not to be receptive to arguments that D will suffer more from the grant of the injunction than P will from its refusal or that the 'public interest' requires the injunction to be withheld.

In determining whether the interference amounts to an actionable nuisance one consideration is the nature of the locality. As it was once said, 'what is a nuisance in Belgrave Square is not necessarily a nuisance in Bermondsey.' This is said not to apply where there is a 'material injury to property.' In the leading case this was physical damage to vegetation caused by copper smelting[52] but it is not very clear whether the same principle applies where there is no physical injury but diminution in value caused by, for example, noise.

It is not clear what the 'permit' is. Statutory authority is a defence to a claim for nuisance if the interference is the inevitable consequence of the authorized activity's

---

50  It is doubtful whether damages for personal injuries are recoverable on the basis of nuisance but even if they are something as evanescent as a headache hardly qualifies. Since the primary remedy is an injunction the point is comparatively unimportant.

51  A house in a beautiful, remote location might well become diminished in value by the construction of another house 200 metres away but that would not be nuisance.

52  *St Helens Smelting Co.* v. *Tipping* (1865) 11 HLC 642.

being carried on with all due care.[53] In modern conditions statutory authority properly so called would normally only be sought for very large scale activities such as the construction of a port or a railway or perhaps a major oil refinery[54], where land has to be compulsorily acquired. Lesser industrial development is likely to be authorized under the town and country planning legislation administered by local authorities. Grant of planning permission does not amount to statutory authority so as to give immunity in nuisance,[55] though it may have an indirect effect by changing the character of a neighbourhood where that is a relevant consideration in determining whether a nuisance exists at common law.[56]

## K. Case 10

(a) The blind man has no action against D because D owes no duty of care to prevent injury to a stranger even if he could do so at no risk or even inconvenience to himself. Negligent acts (including for this purpose omissions which are a part of a course of positive conduct – such as failing to brake while driving) which cause physical damage are generally regarded as legal wrongs; omissions are generally not. The general criminal law is to the same effect. Naturally there are comparatively few cases which raise the issue quite so starkly as this hypothetical but there are numerous statements that the law is so. Although the rule has been criticized by comparison with that prevailing elsewhere[57] it has been firmly restated by the House of Lords in *Stovin* v. *Wise*.[58] In Lord Hoffmann's view[59]

'There are sound reasons why omissions require different treatment from positive conduct. It is one thing for the law to say that a person who undertakes some activity shall take reasonable care not to cause damage to others. It is another thing for the law to require that a person who is doing nothing in particular shall take steps to prevent another from suffering harm from the acts of third parties or natural causes. One can put the matter in political, moral or economic terms. In political terms it is less of an invasion of an individual's freedom for the law to require him to consider the safety of others in his actions than to impose upon him a duty to rescue or protect. A moral version of this point may be called the 'Why pick on me?' argument. A duty to prevent harm to others or to render assistance to a person in danger or distress may apply to a large and indeterminate class of people who happen to be able to do something.

---

53  Of course the statute authorizing the activity may provide for some form of compensation for those injuriously affected.
54  *See Allen* v. *Gulf Oil* [1981] AC 1001 (statutory authority for Milford Haven development).
55  *Hunter* v. *Canary Wharf* [1996] 1 All ER 482; reversed on other grounds [1997] 2 All ER 426.
56  *Gillingham BC* v. *Medway (Chatham) Dock Co.* [1993] QB 343.
57  For example, by Lord Goff in *Smith* v. *Littlewoods* [1987] AC 241.
58  [1997] 3 All ER 801.
59  At 819, Lords Goff and Jauncey concurring. Although Lords Nicholls and Slynn dissented they did not disagree with the basic rule stated by the majority.

Why should one be held liable rather than another? In economic terms, the efficient allocation of resources usually requires an activity should bear its own costs. If it benefits from being able to impose some of its costs on other people (what economists call 'externalities') the market is distorted because the activity appears cheaper than it really is. So liability to pay compensation for loss caused by negligent conduct acts as a deterrent against increasing the cost of the activity to the community and reduces externalities. But there is no similar justification for requiring a person who is not doing anything to spend money on behalf of someone else. Except in special cases (such as marine salvage) English law does not reward someone who voluntarily confers a benefit on another. So there must be some special reason why he should have to put his hand in his pocket.'

As has been said in Australia, 'both priest and levite ensured performance of any common law duty of care to the stricken traveller when, by crossing to the other side of the road they avoided throwing up dust in his wounds'[60]. Many standard relationships (e.g., occupier and visitor, occupier and neighbour, carrier and passenger, employer and employee, gaoler and prisoner and so on) will impose a duty of affirmative action to protect from danger and courts will probably be receptive to arguments that by his conduct a defendant has 'assumed responsibility' for the plaintiff's safety. But, on these stark facts there is nothing upon which to hang such an assumption.

(b) The act of digging the hole clearly imposes a duty to road users to take care (even, so far as practicable, to vulnerable users like blind people) that it does not present a danger. This has initially been fulfilled but there is also a duty to take reasonable steps to maintain the fence in secure condition even if it is damaged by the acts of third parties for whom D is not vicariously liable. If one regards this as an omission a duty of affirmative action is justified by D's creation, albeit lawful, of the potential danger.

(c) General tort law principles would suggest the same answer as in the case of the blind man and the hole in the road and this is probably correct. There is no pre-existing relationship between P and D and no assumption of responsibility by D for P's care. It may be that the regulations governing the National Health Service require general practitioners to give emergency treatment to persons who are not their patients and it is said that in an unreported case in 1955[61] it was *conceded* by the defence that a doctor was under a duty to assist a non-patient in an emergency. It is not obvious why D's contractual duty to X should automatically lead to a tort duty to P when D has simply failed to act. A former reluctance to use the omissions rule to deny liability in public authorities now seem to have been reversed. It has recently been held that the fire brigade is not liable in negligence for failure to turn out to fight a fire or for inadequate performance in fighting it.[62] *Aliter* where by some positive conduct it makes the position

60   Deane J in *Jaensch* v. *Coffey* (1984) 54 ALR 417.
61   *Barnes* v. *Crabtree*.
62   *Capital & Counties* v. *Hampshire CC* [1997] 2 All ER 865.

worse, for example by turning off a sprinkler system. There is no liability based upon assumption of responsibility by attendance at the fire nor one based on general reliance on a public authority carrying out its function.[63] What is now in some doubt is the position where there is detrimental reliance by the plaintiff or by some third party.[64]

## L. Case 11

The transaction between D and P is presumably a contract and a contract of sale of goods.[65] Although English law is ready to accept concurrent liability in contract and tort there could be no tort liability here. The nature of the damage means that it would be outside the scope of Part I of the Consumer Protection Act 1987 (implementing the 1985 Product Liability Directive) even if the Act applied, which it does not because P is in business rather than a consumer. The common law of negligence is almost certainly inapplicable because it does not extend to complaints that goods supplied are inadequate for their purpose: that is the concern of the law of contract.[66] A breach of contract is now regarded as a legal wrong and not merely as the exercise of an option to pay damages for non-performance, but it is not a wrong classified as a tort.[67] It may be said, however, that on the bare facts given P appears to have a good chance of success in his contract action since there would be likely to be an implied term that the goods were reasonably suitable for the purpose for which they were bought and the losses suffered would appear to be within the scope of the normal remoteness principles in contract.

## M. Case 12

Note – I interpret this on the basis that (a) and (b) are cumulative, i.e., I am not required to discuss the contractual position. Part I of the Consumer Protection Act 1987 is inapplicable because although a dog is 'goods' D does not appear to be in any of the categories of persons on whom the Act imposes liability.[68] There is strict liability for damage done by domestic animals which have a dangerous characteristic[69] of which the keeper is aware under s.2 (2) of the Animals act 1971 (replacing broadly similar common law rules). This would be inapplicable if the sale had been effective because when the accident occurred D was no longer the keeper, having sold it to P. However, 'keeper' is

---

63    Compare Mason J in *Sutherland CC* v. *Heyman* (1985) 157 CLR 424.
64    In *OLL* v. *Secretary of State for Transport* [1997] 3 All ER 897 the court rejected a claim against the coastguard based upon alleged negligence in directing a RAF rescue helicopter. *Sed quaere.*
65    The implication is that it is the hardware that is the problem.
66    *Muirhead* v. *Industrial Tank Specialities Ltd* [1986] QB 507.
67    Though a breach of contract may, as unlawful means, provide an element in the torts considered under Cases 1 to 5.
68    Conceivably he could be a supplier who would attract liability if he failed to identify his own supplier. If he did so, there would seem to be equally formidable difficulties in a claim by P against that supplier.
69    Although the subsection is aimed at what might be called 'character defects' in animals it appears wide enough to catch this case.

defined to include 'owner' so if the sale is void presumably no property has passed to P and D is liable.[70] There would also appear to be liability under the general law of negligence since although most of the cases are about manufacturers, there is no doubt that a duty of care is owed by a seller to the buyer where the goods are dangerous.[71]

## N. Case 13

We are not asked directly to consider the position of the manufacturer of the medicine. However, it would seem that he would be liable under Part I of the Consumer Protection Act 1987 since the error in labelling would mean that the drug was 'defective'. In parallel, the error in labelling would seem to produce virtually irresistible evidence of negligence at common law.

As to nurse D and the employers, the clinic or hospital, the injury would no doubt raise a *prima facie* case of negligence (*res ipsa loquitur*) but the incorrect labelling would rebut this unless there was some reason to suspect the label. Most medical treatment in England is given under the National Health Service and there is therefore no contractual relationship between the hospital and the patient. The hospital (but probably not the nurse) has 'supplied' the drug for the purposes of s.3 of the 1987 Act but this liability is easily escaped by identifying the manufacturer. If the hospital is a private one there would be a contractual relationship with the patient which might attract a strict liability under the Supply of Goods and Services Act 1982 in respect of the drug, but this is only really significant if the manufacturer is insolvent since the hospital would be entitled to an indemnity from the manufacturer.

---

70 Having been involved in the preparation of this legislation I can testify even after 27 years that this was a contingency that was not foreseen!

71 *Kubach* v. *Hollands* [1937] 3 All ER 907; *cf. Hurley* v. *Dyke* [1979] RTR 265 (goods sold 'as seen'). There are old cases to the effect that a gratuitous transferor is not liable but (a) it would seem wrong to regard D as a gratuitous transferor and (b) the cases are probably inconsistent with the modern development of the law of negligence.

# France

## Le 'Wrongfulness' en Droit Français

## Geneviève Viney

## I.  Réponses aux Questions

### A.  Réponse à la Question 'Is there a Requirement of 'Wrongfulness' in French Law?'

La condition de 'faute' est expressément mentionnée à l'article 1382 du code civil.

Cette condition est très vivante dans de nombreux domaines, mais elle a été a peu près écartée en ce qui concerne les accidents corporels par une responsabilité sans faute très largement définie.

En outre, la faute n'est pas nécessairement personnelle. La responsabilité du fait d'autrui s'est beaucoup développée.

Enfin, la faute est définie aujourd'hui d'une manière purement objective, comme un comportement défectueux, sans référence au discernement (puisqu'elle peut être imputée à un inconscient). Ce comportement défectueux recouvre non seulement la méconnaissance d'une règle impérative imposée par une loi ou un règlement (cette infraction à la légalité objective étant nécessairement une faute), mais aussi toutes sortes d'actes ou d'omissions que le juge assimile à des fautes parce qu'il les juge contraires à la norme générale de comportement que l'on peut attendre d'un individu raisonnable (le bon père de famille) dans la situation où il s'est trouvé.

En droit français, l'illicéité n'est pas un élément distinct de la faute: les deux notions sont confondues.

La faute délictuelle n'est pas 'relative'. Elle n'est pas un manquement à un *duty of care*' n'existant qu'entre telle et telle personne. En cela, elle s'oppose à l'inexécution contractuelle (ou faute contractuelle).

Le droit civil français ne fait qu'une place très réduite à la notion de '*Schutznorm*' (sélection des intérêts protégés par telle ou telle règle de comportement).

*H. Koziol (ed.), Unification of Tort Law: Wrongfulness*, 57–64.
©1998 *Kluwer Law International. Printed in The Netherlands.*

B.   *Réponse à la Question: 'Is wrongfulness one of the conditions of an actionable tort and is it a reason for rejecting an actionable tort?'*

Je pense que l'on pourrait mettre en avant la notion de 'comportement raisonnable ou normal eu égard aux circonstances dans lesquelles s'est trouvé placé le sujet', en indiquant que ce comportement raisonnable implique un degré de prudence et de diligence inégal selon les intérêts en cause, ce qui permettrait de justifier des règles de responsabilité différentes en fonction de la nature du dommage causé (par exemple, en matière de sécurité des personnes, un degré de diligence très élevé, fondé sur le 'principe de précaution' serait requis alors que la diligence imposée quant à la sécurité des biens pourrait être moins exigeante).

C.   *'What reasons or factors are to be taken into account in establishing or denying liability?'*

1. La gravité de la faute
Il est normal, à mon avis, que la faute intentionnelle et même la faute lourde soit une cause d'aggravation de la responsabilité.
     Je vois deux possibilités d'aménager cette aggravation:
–    Tenir en échec les limitations de responsabilité prévues par une clause contractuelle ou par un texte légal ou réglementaire en présence d'une telle faute (c'est la solution du droit français);
–    Autoriser le prononcé de 'dommages et intérêts punitifs' (ils sont actuellement interdits en droit français, mais leur introduction serait concevable).

2. La nature de l'acte en cause
Danger de la chose utilisée ou de l'activité exercée.

(i)   Je pense que cela justifie l'application de régimes de responsabilité sans faute (*strict liability*) ou, à défaut, une appréciation stricte de la faute, incluant le 'principe de précaution' (le simple doute scientifique sur la sécurité imposant l'abstention).

(ii)  *Interférence avec le contrat.*
      Lorsqu'un même fait atteint de la même façon un cocontractant et un tiers, il parait logique d'admettre le même régime de responsabilité au profit de l'un et de l'autre (ce n'est pas le cas actuellement en droit français où existe une distinction rigide entre responsabilité contractuelle et responsabilité délictuelle).

(iii) *Responsabilité du fait des produits défectueux.*
      Le régime admis par la directive européenne du 25 juillet 1985 au profit des victimes non professionnelles devrait être également au profit des professionnels (notamment des sociétés).

(iv) *Diffamation, délits de presse.*

Ici, il faut tenir compte du principe de liberté de la presse et, plus généralement, de la liberté d'expression, ce qui entraîne une appréciation de la faute plus indulgente: La responsabilité doit être cantonnée au cas d'abus de cette liberté.

(v) *Abus du droit.*

On retrouve la même considération. L'existence d'un droit crée, pour son titulaire, une certaine zone d'irresponsabilité qui est d'ailleurs très difficile à délimiter (faut il limiter l'abus du droit à son exercice dans l'intention de nuire à autrui, ou faire intervenir la notion de finalité des droits subjectifs et l'admettre en cas d'exercice incorrect du droit? La question n'est pas clairement tranchée en droit français, 'l'abus' étant admis plus facilement pour certains droits que pour d'autres).

(vi) *Responsabilité professionnelle.*

Le caractère professionnel de l'activité est un facteur d'aggravation de la responsabilité car le professionnel se prévaut d'une compétence particulière dans sa spécialité et de ce fait il crée une 'attente légitime' chez ceux qui s'adressent à lui.

Cela justifie d'abord une appréciation stricte de la compétence requise.

Cela entraîne également l'admission de devoirs ou d'obligations professionnelles spécifiques, qui sont liées à cette compétence particulière, par exemple les obligations d'information, de mise en garde et de conseil.

Ces obligations professionnelles sont souvent rattachées à un contrat (conclu entre le professionnel et son client), mais elles ne sont pas strictement contractuelles et sont source de responsabilité à l'égard de toute personne qui fait appel au professionnel ou qui profite directement ou indirectement des prestations qu'il fournit. Il serait souhaitable que le régime de responsabilité appliqué en cas de manquement à ces devoirs professionnels soit le même, quelle que soit la victime – cocontractant ou tiers – (voir *supra*).

(vii) *Accidents du travail.*

En droit français, il existe pour ces accidents un régime particulier d'indemnisation intégré au régime général de la Sécurité sociale et très largement indépendant de la responsabilité. Les prestations sont versées par la caisse de sécurité sociale sans recherche préalable des responsabilités.

Toutefois ce régime, qui n'assure qu'une indemnisation partielle et forfaitaire, est parfois complété par la mise en jeu de la responsabilité de l'employeur, en cas de faute intentionnelle ou de faute inexcusable de celui-ci ou de certains de ses préposés.

Le particularisme du droit des accidents du travail, et, en tout cas, l'élimination de la condition de la faute pour accorder une indemnisation minimale, me parait nécessaire et irréversible.

3. La nature du dommage
J'estime qu'elle devrait être prise en compte pour apprécier la faute requise (voir réponse aux questions N° 2 et 3).
    Ce n'est pas le cas actuellement en droit français.

4. 'Floodgates argument'
Cet argument me parait dangereux car il manque totalement de rigueur.
    Il n'a guère d'impact actuellement sur la jurisprudence française.

5. Existence de plusieurs responsables
Elle engendre l'obligation 'in solidum' (au tout) de chacun des co-responsables vis-à-vis de la victime.
    En ce qui concerne la contribution définitive (recours entre co-responsables), la gravité de la faute est prise en compte et joue un rôle important.

6. Existence d'une assurance couvrant le responsable ou la victime
Théoriquement cette circonstance n'a pas d'influence sur la responsabilité, mais en fait elle est souvent déterminante pour le juge qui statue sur l'affaire.
    Il arrive également que les tribunaux estiment que le défaut d'assurance de l'auteur du dommage ou le fait de n'avoir par averti les personnes que l'on expose à un risque de l'absence d'assurance est une faute d'imprudence justifiant la responsabilité.

7. Les implications de la responsabilité pour les assureurs et l'assurabilité
C'est un facteur qui est partout sous-jacent et qui explique de très nombreuses solutions légales ou jurisprudentielles concernant la désignation du ou des responsables, même s'il n'est pas officiellement mis en avant par les juges.

8. Le coût des précautions à prendre
C'est un facteur d'appréciation de la faute.

9. La qualité de professionnel du défendeur ou de la victime
Le professionnel est chargé de responsabilités plus lourdes que le non professionnel (voir supra).
    Le fait que la victime soit un professionnel peut également avoir une incidence sur la responsabilité, notamment lorsque celle-ci repose sur le manquement au devoir d'information ou de conseil car celui-ci est moins strict à l'égard d'un professionnel, réputé compétent.

10. La prévisibilité du dommage
C'est un facteur d'appréciation de la faute (comme d'ailleurs de la causalité).

## II. Cas Pratiques

### A. 1er cas

P. pourrait agir en concurrence déloyale contre D. et il aurait des chances d'obtenir une condamnation car les circonstances sont de nature à établir qu'il a agi dans leu seul but de provoquer la faillite de P. (intention de nuire).

### B. 2e cas

P. peut agir en responsabilité contre X. et contre D. pour complicité dans la violation de l'accord d'exclusivité. Il a des chances d'obtenir la condamnation de D. à condition de prouver que celui-ci connaissait l'accord passé avec X. lorsqu'il a sollicité la diva.

### C. 3e cas

X. peut théoriquement agir contre Y. sur le terrain de la responsabilité délictuelle pour faute, mais il y a peu de chance qu'il parvienne à établir avec certitude que si Y. avait respecté le feu, l'ordre d'arrivée aurait été inverse. L'action risque donc d'échouer faute de preuve de la causalité.

### D. 4e cas

P. peut agir contre D. sur le fondement de la responsabilité délictuelle pour faute et il a des chances sérieuses d'obtenir réparation car la faute parait caractérisée.

### E. 5e cas

La responsabilité de D. est engagée vis à vis de P. à qui *il a fait perdre* par sa faute *une chance sérieuse* d'obtenir le marché (responsabilité délictuelle pour faute).

### F. 6e cas

B n'encourt normalement aucune responsabilité, sauf si A parvient à établir que l'article n'a été écrit que dans le seul but de lui nuire.

### G. 7e cas

Si D a menti, il est incontestablement responsable vis à vis de P pour les conséquences de sa faute. En revanche, si l'appréciation est fondée sur des faits objectivement établis, le juge devra rechercher si l'ancien employeur a fait preuve ou non d'une sévérité excessive et de légèreté dans l'information donnée. En cas de réponse positive, la responsabilité sera engagée.

## H. 8e cas

Une action est possible mais, en droit français, elle serait plutôt située sur le terrain contractuel (le restaurant assument, vis-à-vis de ses clients, une obligation de sécurité de moyens pendant qu'ils se trouvent dans le restaurant).

En ce qui concerne la faute, les juges l'apprécieront en fonction des témoignages des autres clients et des indices objectifs. Il me semble que le patron du restaurant a fait preuve en l'espèce au moins de maladresse. Or la maladresse est assez souvent assimilée à une faute surtout si elle est commise par un professionnel et parait incompatible avec le comportement requis d'un bon professionnel.

Toutefois, je pense qu'en l'occurrence la responsabilité ne serait pas intégrale car le juge tendrait vraisemblablement compte de la faute concurrente de la victime, si du moins le défendeur peut prouver que, par son attitude agressive ou tout simplement par son ivresse, V. a contribué à la réalisation du dommage.

## I. 9e cas

Il s'agit là d'un cas-type d'application de la théorie des troubles de voisinage qui est, en droit français, une *responsabilité sans faute*, la seule condition de cette responsabilité étant *le caractère excessif ou anormal du trouble causé aux voisins*.

L'existence ou l'absence d'une autorisation pour exercer l'activité professionnelle ne change rien à la responsabilité de l'industriel, le principe étant que les autorisations administratives sont données 'sous réserce des droits des tiers'.

En principe, A, B et C pourront obtenir réparation de leur dommage à condition de prouver que l'odeur dégagée dépasse, pour eux, la mesure des inconvénients ordinaires du voisinage. C'est une question de niveau objectif de la nuisance et non pas de nature du dommage, le préjudice d'agrément (subi par A) étant susceptible de justifier une réparation, tout comme le dommage corporel (subi par B) et la perte économique (subie par C).

Il n'est pas tenu compte de la sensibilité particulière de la victime.

En revanche, l'industriel pourrait éventuellement se prévaloir (pour échapper à sa responsabilité) du fait que telle ou telle des victimes est venue s'installer à proximité de son installation alors que celle-ci présentait déjà les mêmes inconvénients.

## J. 10e cas

(a)  Le fait de n'avoir pas fait un geste pour empêcher l'aveugle de tomber dans le trou est une faute, si D pouvait accomplir ce geste sans danger pour lui-même ou pour autrui.

(b)  Le fait de n'avoir pas réagi à l'information que la clôture avait été retirée peut être une négligence fautive, si ce fait était vraisemblable et que D. pouvait sans trop de difficulté revenir sur place pour la remettre. En revanche, à défaut de ces conditions, le juge pourrait considérer qu'il n'y a pas de faute.

(c)  Le refus d'assistance du médecin est une faute qui est même pénalement sanctionnée et qui peut faire l'objet de poursuites disciplinaires.

## K. 11e cas

En droit français, il s'agit ici d'une responsabilité contractuelle pour manquement à l'obligation de conseil du vendeur professionnel. Cette responsabilité est admise.

## L. 12e cas

L'acheteur a la possibilité d'exercer deux actions:
–  Une action en nullité de la vente pour erreur sur une qualité essentielle de l'animal vendu.
–  Une action en responsabilité: l'action en responsabilité sera de nature contractuelle si l'action en nullité n'est pas exercée.

Elle sera de nature délictuelle si la nullité est demandée et prononcée. Elle pourra alors être fondée soit sur l'article 1382 c.c. (responsabilité pour faute) soit sur l'article 1385 (responsabilité du fait de l'animal).

L'action contractuelle aboutira à une condamnation s'il est établi que le vendeur connaissait l'état du chien ou s'il s'agit d'un vendeur professionnel (qui est censé connaître les vices de l'animal vendu).

Quant à l'action délictuelle pour faute (article 1382), son succès est subordonné à la preuve que P. connaissait le défaut de l'animal ou qu'il aurait pu le connaître par un examen plus attentif. Dans ces deux hypothèses il a en effet commis une faute d'imprudence en le remettant à un éventuel acheteur. Certains arrêts ont également admis que le vendeur professionnel qui met sur le marché un produit défectueux commet ainsi une faute délictuelle.

Je n'examinerai pas ici la possibilité d'invoquer contre le vendeur le régime spécial de responsabilité du fait de l'animal prévu par l'article 1385 du code civil car il s'agit d'une responsabilité sans faute. Indiquons simplement que le succès de cette action contre le vendeur dépend du point de savoir si celui-ci, malgré la vente, avait conservé la 'garde' de l'animal au moment où celui-ci a causé le dommage.

## M. 13e cas

Dans cette hypothèse, la responsabilité incombe principalement au laboratoire qui a mal dosé et mal étiqueté le médicament.
Toute autre personne dont la responsabilité serait retenue (l'infirmière ou son commettant, c'est-à-dire l'hôpital ou la clinique pour laquelle elle travaille) aurait un recours contre ce laboratoire sur le fondement du manquement à l'obligation d'information.

Est-il cependant envisageable de retenir également la responsabilité provisoire de l'infirmière vis à vis de la victime?

Sur le terrain de la responsabilité pour faute, la réponse me parait négative car le comportement de l'infirmière a été normal.

En revanche, il n'est pas inconcevable qu'elle soit tenue pour responsable du défaut du produit qu'elle a utilisé, à condition toutefois qu'il s'agisse d'une infirmière indépendante venue au domicile du patient. Si, au contraire, elle a agi pour le compte d'un hôpital ou d'une clinique en tant que salariée, cette responsabilité pèserait alors sur le commettant.

# Greece

WRONGFULNESS UNDER GREEK LAW

Konstantinos D. Kerameus

## I.  General Information

1.   As far as the question is concerned whether there is a requirement of 'wrongfulness' in Greek law, please refer to the Hellenic National Report on European Tort Law published in *Limits of Liability*, 1996, p.43, where an attempt to limit Greek law of tort has been made by Prof. K. Roussos and myself. In this present report I will assess the matter of the unlawful character of negligent behaviour, as delictual liability has already been analyzed in the aforesaid study.

2.   More specifically under Greek law in order to assess the liability of the debtor, his fault is of crucial significance. By 'fault' the law means the bond which exists between a person and an action or its result, which justifies the imputation of blame to him. There are two degrees of fault, depending upon its gravity: wilful conduct (*dolus*) and negligence. The latter case is the significant one for this present report and it exists when the culprit did not wish the result but he did not devote the care which he could and ought to have given to the averting of the (unlawful) result. In the aforesaid study the difficulties in distinguishing 'unlawfulness' from 'culpability' were pointed out in detail and it was clearly stated that the classical Greek doctrine[1] and the prevailing case law tend to give a negative answer to the question of whether negligence may in itself qualify as 'illegal' behaviour and thus establish delictual liability, regardless of any specific provision which might prohibit that behaviour.

3.   In spite of the above concerns, there are two ways of approaching the culprit's conduct in order to see if the same was careful or not and whether the unlawful result could be foreseen or not: the subjective and the objective one.

(a)  Pursuant to the subjective point of view it is crucial to examine the culprit's ability to understand that what he was doing could have an unlawful result, i.e., the culprit's profession, experience and mental health are important in this case. If the culprit did not act in accordance with the care which he himself could have displayed, he will be deemed

---

1    *See* references in the following note of the study.

*H. Koziol (ed.), Unification of Tort Law: Wrongfulness*, 65–68.
©1998 *Kluwer Law International. Printed in The Netherlands.*

to have been negligent. By contrast, if he did, he will not be considered as acting negligently, even if other people would have shown greater care. The subjective criterion is prevailing in criminal law.

(b)  In Greek civil law, however, another criterion, the objective one, prevails. In other words, the capabilities of the average prudent and conscientious man is what is regarded as important for judging whether a conduct is negligent or not. The deviation of the conduct of the culprit from those capabilities constitutes negligence, even if he himself was not able to behave in another way. Therefore, if the culprit because of his exceptional abilities is capable of acting with a greater care and attention, he will not be regarded as negligent, as this greater attention does not correspond to the capabilities of the average prudent man. The above has been incorporated in Article 330 sent. 2 of the Greek Civil Code (CC) which states that: negligence exists where the care required by business has not been exercised. The Greek Supreme Court,[2] as already pointed out in the aforesaid study on the matter, has opted for that criterion more than once.

4.   In view of the above, negligence is prohibited as a way of behaving because there is objective disapprobation of the negligent act and therefore the said act is deemed to be unlawful. The conduct in other words is treated as a type of fault on the grounds that the person concerned should have foreseen and avoided the violation which has occurred. The mere fact that the culprit could foresee the violation turns his act into unlawful. In this way the same act (negligent act) may constitute at the same time an unlawful conduct and a conduct at fault since as the fact that the said person was able to foresee and avoid the violation may equally, pursuant to the above, establish fault. This was also admitted by the aforementioned decisions of the Greek Supreme Court which have considered that the departure from normal standards of care constitutes a sufficient feature of unlawfulness. As explained above, this does not mean, however, that a negligent behaviour by itself gives birth to delictual liability as well.

## II. The Cases

Please note that I have given comments rather than 'clear-cut' answers to the questions raised by the cases.

### A. Case 1

The answer would be most probably handled by the rules of unfair competition (L. 146/19). Unlawfulness in the above sense does not appear to apply here.

---

2    *Areios Pagos* 183-186/1987, HellDni 29 (1988) 492 (493 II); 81/1991, HellDni 32 (1991) 1215 (1216 I).

## B. Case 2

Failure to perform a contractual obligation has an objective character and by itself does not justify personal censure to the debtor. It is imputed to him only objectively. For example, the thing owed is destroyed by a third party. This is not, however, the case here. D seems to have acted against the principle of good faith (CC 281), by inducing X to breach her contract with P. Contractual liability of X may also be established.

## C. Case 3

There would be no claim. The breach of such statutory duty gives a claim only to a representative of the state, i.e., a policeman, or to a counterpart if a contract exists.

## D. Case 4

There would be no claim in accordance with Greek tort rules.

## E. Case 5

Apart from fraud from the side of D against the Minister, P could sue the Minister and ask for compensation, if he thinks that the Minister ought to have known the dishonest character of the representations made by D.

## F. Case 6

The answer should be given in the negative as the criminal past of A is a reality and therefore B said the truth.

## G. Case 7

A claim exists under general tort law, if it can be proved that the information given in the reference is not true (CC 920).

## H. Case 8

The answer should be given in the affirmative under CC 929.

## I. Case 9

The fact that O has or does not have a permit is not significant for the application of Article 929 CC (personal injury). As far as the value of the house is concerned, if O has a permit there is no claim; by contrast, if O does not have a permit Article 1003 CC shall apply whereby the effects of smoke, exhalations, heat, noise and other similar affections caused by a property to another should be tolerated, as long as the use of the affected property is not severely infringed or these affects are due to the regular use of the properties in the area.

## J.  Case 10

10a: Perhaps criminal but no civil liability.

10b: Under Article 929 CC and in view of the fact that there is a causal link between the damage and the act (or omission), D could be held liable.

10c: The only precedent[3] found among the Supreme Court's cases with respect to medical liability[4] has dealt with the matter of medical negligence shown during an operation. We could, however, draw from the said case the conclusion that, whenever a doctor shows negligence in practising his profession, he becomes liable towards his patient.

## K. Case 11

Contractual liability is established under the circumstances described by this case.

## L. Case 12

If the contract is valid contractual liability is established; by contrast if the contract is null and void, liability on the grounds of CC 929 may be established.

## M. Case 13

Liability of the medicament's manufacturer may be established easily in this case.

---

3   *Areios Pagos* 1356/1991, HellDni 33 (1992) 1192.
4   *See* Fountedaki, 'The problem of causal link in medical liability', HellDni 35 (1994) 1226.

# Italy

'Wrongfulness' in the Italian Legal System

Francesco D. Busnelli and Giovanni Comandé

## I. Wrongfulness in the 1942 Italian Civil Code

Wrongfulness in Italy's legal system was codified in the 1942 Civil Code, Art. 2043 general norm on torts. The provision states that 'any intentional or negligent act, that causes *wrongful damage*[1] to others, must be compensated for by the wrongdoer'.

This use of the term 'wrongfulness' '*ingiustizia del danno*' is innovative with respect to Art. 1151 of the 1865 Civil Code. This code, by literally translating Napoleon Code Art. 1382, stated that 'any act that causes damage to others compels the person guilty of the act to compensate the damage'. A divergency was created between the norm based on the French model and its interpretation based on the German model. This interpretation considered Art. 1151 as a sanctioning norm of torts specifically regulated by other norms (sanctioning and typifying norm[2]).

The introduction of wrongfulness in the 1942 Code initially strengthened the influence of the German model because the concept of wrongfulness, although set literally alongside the category of damage, was connected to the illegal act. So even Art. 2043 of the Civil Code is rewritten as a secondary provision aimed at sanctioning, with compensation remedy, torts typified and specifically characterized by wrongfulness through other norms in the legal system.

The German-inspired concept of sanctioning and typifying the civil illegal act is confirmed even though there is a divergency between the wording of Art. 2043 C.C. and that of paragraph 823 BGB and in spite of the fact that the original intention of the legislator was to create an intermediate model between the general clause of the French legal system and the rigid typicality of the German system.

---

1    The italics are added in the original copy.
2    *See* in particular, Carnelutti, *Il danno e il reato* (1926), Padova, p. 62.

69

*H. Koziol (ed.), Unification of Tort Law: Wrongfulness, 69–81.*
©1998 *Kluwer Law International. Printed in The Netherlands.*

Twenty years after the Code was issued, the innovative meaning of the category of wrongfulness is perceived, because wrongfulness is referred to the damage[3] rather than to the act. Contemporarily, a functional concept of indemnity as compensation rather than sanction is accepted. Through this new approach a more flexible interpretation of Art. 2043 is introduced. This norm is sometimes considered a general and atypical clause and sometimes a general rule. In any case it is placed in an intermediate position between, on the one hand, giving unlimited power to the judge in recognizing any interest declared by the damaged party and, on the other hand, delegating complete power to the legislator to typify the damaged interest or the tort. The judge can recognize the right to compensation for the damaged interests that are in the legal system and therefore are worthy of compensation. In this manner, it is possible to have a progressive and controlled expansion in the area of civil liability thanks to a primary norm whose content is a sort of balanced mediation between the French model (and more recently, the Dutch model) and the German concept.

## II. Wrongfulness as a Condition for Taking Action against the Illegal Act

The flexibility of the wrongfulness clause is clearly revealed in its technical nature.

From a technical juridical point of view, wrongfulness is shown as the condition needed to take action against civil torts and it has two aspects: that of damage to a juridically important interest (damage *contra ius*) and that of the unjustifiable nature of the conduct (damage *non iure*).

Scholar[4] has initially focused its attention on the first aspect. The new interpretation of Art. 2043 has extended the damage *contra ius* from damage to absolute rights to that of damage to right to have the obligation performed, caused not by the debtor but by a third person (*ius in personam*).

This evolution was linked to two interventions by the Courts: the *Superga manslaughter* case in 1953[5] for the death of Turin's football team in a plane crash and the 1971[6] *Meroni manslaughter* case for the death of a Turin football player in a car crash. Both resulted in credit damage to the Turin Football Association. These two cases reveal that the Supreme Court initially refused to protect the right but at a later stage it recognized the right to compensation for damage to right to have the obligation performed, caused not by the debtor but by a third person.

Through this evolution and thanks to scholars' attention to this theme, the following rule has been accepted: the right to compensation for damage by violating the right to

---

3   *See*, in particular, Rodotá, *Il problema della responsabilitá civile* (1964), Milano, spec. 132. Before this came out we must point out that several authors, while still referring wrongfulness to the act, had at the same time created hermeneutic expedients to free the norm from the constraints of typicality and sanction: Sacco, 'L'ingiustizia di cui all'art' 2043 c.c., in: Foro pad. 1960, I, 1420 and Schlesinger, 'La ingiustizia del danno nell'illecito civile', in: Jus 1960, 336 ff.

4   *See* Busnelli, *La lesione del credito da parte di terzi* (1964), Milano, *passim*.

5   Cass., 4 luglio 1953, n. 2085, in: Foro it. 1953, I, 1087 ff.

6   Cass., 29 marzo 1978, n. 1459, in: Foro it. 1978, I, 833 ff.

have the obligation performed caused by a third person can only be recognized if the loss is complete and irreparable.

Above and beyond the two categories of absolute rights and relative personal rights (there is a tendency to favour the right to compensation for both), we can find differing opinions on the possible extension of the clause on wrongfulness. In particular, while the doctrine seems to be more favourable towards an ulterior extension of the application field of wrongfulness, the Courts remain faithful to the traditional rule and even create fictitious rights.

In light of these opposing views, the more correct approach seems to be that which tends to verify, through the wrongfulness of damage, the existence of damage to interests worthy of being compensated, in that they are juridically important according to the rules and principles of the legal system.

Among the interests that can be included in the clause on the wrongfulness of damage, we must above all mention what we call in Italy 'rightful interest', that is, the interest of the person in the correct (and therefore legitimate) conduct of public administration. The two theses on this interest seem unacceptable: one considers damage to 'rightful interest' consistently wrongful and the other considers this damage generically excluded from the damage *contra ius*. We must accept an intermediate definition that recognizes the wrongful nature in the damage to a 'rightful interest' on certain conditions. These conditions arise when the 'rightful interest' presents itself as a 'right awaiting expansion'. This, for example, happens when the Public Administration illegitimately denies the owner the licence to build on his property.[7] In other cases these conditions do not exist (compare no. 3).

In the area of interests worthy of the right to compensation we can also include all the hypotheses on damage to a legitimate juridical expectancy. Take for example the case of damage to a person heir to a will that is void through fault of the notary, or the hypotheses of damage to possession without property, or damage caused by loss of legal alimony because the debtor is killed.

Finally, when we reach the last frontier of civil liability we come to the area of damage caused by inexact information. Doctrine has tried to define a criterion for when such an interest must be compensated.[8] This criterion is found in the 'damage caused by breach of trust towards a person who couldn't see the error' and it is deduced from a precise indication in the rules of the Civil Code (Art. 1337 and Art. 1338) and from the special rules on the products liability.

It therefore seems clear that the problem of damage *contra ius* is no longer that of placing an interest in a particular right (*ein sonstiges Recht*) but of evaluating if the interest must be compensated in that it is juridically important on the basis of the rules and principles of the legal system.

After examining the fundamental features of the conditions for taking action against illegal acts, with reference to damage *contra ius*, we must now analyze the other element

---

7   *See* Busnelli, 'Illecito civile', in: *Enciclopedia Giuridica Treccani* (1991), Roma, p. 13.
8   *See* Busnelli, 'Itinerari europei nella "terra di nessuno tra contratto e fatto illecito": la responsabilitá da informazioni inesatte', in: *Contratto impresa* 1991, 2, 561.

that constitutes wrongfulness (damage *non iure*), that is, the lack of justifications that render behaviour legal and therefore not wrongful. Justifications, in the civil system, orbit around the exercise of a right which does not exclude the importance of other justifications (fulfilment of a duty, informed consent, legitimate defence, necessity, lawful use of weapons) among which legitimate defence and necessity are mentioned in Art. 2044 and Art. 2045.

Before discussing the hypotheses that can reject the compensation request, we must refer to those hypotheses that are apparently part of the justification of the exercise of a right but in reality they are removed from the category of legitimacy because they are an abuse of right.

The abuse of right is the issue of a controversial dogmatic restructuring in that it has not been codified in a general content provision. Nevertheless, according to the present scholar, its importance must be recognized because the principle is found in various rules of the Civil Code, such as objective good faith as well as the prohibition of emulative acts. Indeed, there have been proposals to include the abuse of right in a prevalently subjective framework (linked to the subjective condition of malice and sometimes of gross negligence), but the concept of abuse of right in an objective sense (linked to objective good faith and emulative acts) is prevalently and dogmatically preferable.

The abuse of right, which is the principle on the basis of which the exercise of a right must compare itself to other areas of interests, is strongly confirmed and fully re-evaluated through the wrongfulness of damage, which is a moderation rule between opposing interests. The field concerning abuse of right has its main application when there are opposing interests that are on an equal level. This deals with the potential contraposition between the exercise of freedom in the extended and atypifying sense (for example, freedom of speech) and damage to rights (moral rights, such as honour, privacy etc.) not susceptible to mere typifying material aggression (for example in cases of damage to property interests or damage to right to health). The conflict that must be faced here in terms of wrongfulness requires a balance of interests (given the abstract equivalence between the conflicting interests). Its solution must be entrusted to the objective and elastic criteria of the abuse of right which are principally connected to canons of objective good faith. Moreover, we must point out that in the conflict between freedom of speech and honour the Courts have concretely defined the balance of interests and the canon of abuse of right through detailed criteria such as: the truth of information, its social use and the correctness of the words used.

## III. The Defect of Wrongfulness as the Reason for Refusing Compensation

The same factors that are outlined, through wrongfulness, as conditions for taking action against illegal acts can also represent possible reasons for denying the right to compensation. Specifically, the lack of damage to an interest of compensation or an appeal to a cause of justification can induce a refusal of action against civil liability.

With respect to the area of damage *contra ius*, the denial of a compensation request is above all justified if the case is a case of damage to a 'rightful interest' (*see* the above-mentioned section II), which is not 'a right awaiting expansion', but rather a mere loss of chance. Let us consider, for example, the case of damage to a participant in a competition caused by the violation of rules by the members of the commission.

Generally, the many possible hypotheses of loss of chance do not have the requisites for the wrongfulness: these hypotheses could range from the damage to the school career of a student after a road accident[9] to damage to an employee who does not get a longed-for promotion.[10]

Similarly, the hypotheses in which there is damage to expectations that have a factual and not juridical importance are not included in the wrongfulness of damage (consider some hypotheses of patrimonial damages caused by murder not connected to loss of actual expectations juridically important).

Finally, in more general terms we must exclude the wrongfulness *contra ius* if there is an economic loss not connected to damage to a juridically important interest according to the rules and principles of the legal system. It is clear that the attempts to recognise the right to take action for compensation in such cases aim to deprive wrongfulness of its full meaning and of its moderating role in opposing interests (between person damaged and damager). These attempts must without doubt be criticized.

If we now come to the element of damage *non iure*, it is clear (as was earlier illustrated) that resorting to one of the causes of justification determines the inevitable refusal of compensation requests. Nevertheless, an independent consideration is due for the justification of necessity whose integration. This justification even if it is true that it leads to a refusal of compensation requests, also allows us to recognize an indemnity right which is determined, according to Art. 2045, by the fair decision of the judge under criteria of equity.

## IV. Answers to the Hypotheticals

Most of the cases have a clear-cut yes/no answer. However, it is difficult to clearly explain all the factors concurring in the decision. Hence we will focus on the wrongfulness requirement, especially in those cases in which it is not entirely clear if it would subsist or not.

## A. Case 1

The first case is a challenging one. D's conduct apparently does not violate any legal rule, besides the fact that his new business is intended only to vindicate his wife's betrayal. His conduct does not constitute a specific tort. However, by ruthlessly under-

---

9    Trib. Lucca, 26 settembre 1990, in: Arch. circ. 1993, 341.
10   Cass., 28 maggio 1992, n. 6392, in: Foro. it. 1993, I, 488; Cass., 11 giugno 1992, n. 7210, in: Giur. it. 1993, I, 1, 1302.

cutting his prices he is not competing for his business but trying to get rid of his wife's lover. In fact, P clearly receives damages from D's conduct causing P's business to go bankrupt.

Certainly, D's way of competing constitutes a violation of Art. 2598 n. 3 c.c.[11] This article contains a pretty detailed hypothesis of conducts contrary to good faith and business fairness. The rule refers to acts that, even though legal, are intended to damage another person's enterprise in violation of business fairness and with fraudulent means, tricks and deceptions to mislead the free choice of clients.[12] Hypothesis number 3 of this article of the code is an elastic rule useful in covering all kinds of unfair competition that constitute a violation of business fairness principles. Note, however, that incorrectness is not a mere violation of ethical principles which is a too indeterminate criteria, but it coincides with non-conformity to the economic system as regulated and interpreted by the legal system as a whole.[13] Hence professional incorrectness should be functionally inferred from the whole manoeuvre to damage competitors. According to this, P can consequently claim damages. In fact, price undercutting is a fair means of competition if it is justified by profit or cost reduction. Otherwise it misleads consumers by infringing the business rules upon which every businessman trusts:[14] D's ruthlessly undercutting his prices is *de facto* a dumping[15] conduct.

In any event, even though D's reduced prices could not violate competition laws, we could still say that D's conduct is illicit. D's violation of professional honesty rules may tinge his conduct with wrongfulness, allowing P to claim damages according to general principles of tort law.[16] According to Article 2043 c.c.[17] damages must be wrongful (caused *non iure* and *contra ius*): they must satisfy two requirements. 'Caused *non iure*' means that a wrongdoer must not pursue an interest worthy of legal protection. 'Caused *contra ius*' means that his conduct must harm an interest worthy of legal protection. According to the story, D's factual interest does not deserve protection. On the contrary, P's interest in doing his business in compliance with the usual rules of fair

---

11  2598 c.c. (Ferme) Besides norms concerning patent and copyright, anybody commits an act of unfair competition if he or she:
  1. uses names or distinctive marks similar to names or distinctive marks lawfully used by others, competitor's producer, or does with any other means acts apt to create confusion with the products or the business of a competitor;
  2. propagates news or remarks on the products or the business of a competitor apt to throw discredit on them, or attributes himself competitor's enterprise or products worthiness;
  3. uses directly or indirectly any other means conforming to principles of business correctness and apt to damage other enterprises (aziende).

12  *See* Corte Appello Trieste, 31 gennaio 1980, in: *Rivista di diritto industriale* 1981, II, 126.

13  For this interpretation *see* Tribunale Verona, 28 dicembre 1985, in: *Giurisprudenza annotata di diritto industriale* 1986, 294. But *see* also Tribunale Catania, 15 maggio 1990, in: *Giurisprudenza annotata di diritto industriale* 1990, 524, that interprets professional correctness as entrepreneurial deontological correctness.

14  *See* Cassazione 1983, n. 2743, in: *Giurisprudenza annotata di diritto industriale* 1983, 72.

15  Tribunale Milano, 28 marzo 1991, in: *Giurisprudenza annotata di diritto industriale* 1991, 460.

16  For more detailed information about the elements of liability required from Article 2043 c.c., *see* our previous report in J. Spier (ed.), *The Limits of Expanding Liability* (1998), p. 137 ff.

17  Article 2043 c.c. Any wilful or negligent act that causes wrongful damages binds whoever committed the act to compensate the damage.

competition seems worthy of it. However, we do not need this construction since both P and D are competitors in the hairdressing business, Article 2598 c.c. plainly applies. Nevertheless, it is useful to mention it in order to explain how the wrongfulness requirement works.

## B. Case 2

In order to give protection, jurisprudence often creates 'new' (i.e., not yet typified) rights, instead of following the more coherent style of qualifying the wrongfulness requirement according to specific principles of law. In any event, judges protect the right to have an obligation performed,[18] as in our hypothetical, but the idea of protecting interests unrecognized as legal rights is not settled yet.

D is clearly interfering with a contractual relationship, by knowing, we suppose, its existence. According to the general principles of tort law he is clearly liable because he is stimulating X to breach her contract with P.[19] This constitutes a violation of P's right to X's performance making D liable for damages. Our courts have reached this conclusion in recent years following innovative scholars' ideas aimed to overcome the usual limitations of the wrongfulness requirement in the injury of absolute vested rights (for example, property and human rights).[20] In fact, now the performance of an obligation may be violated by a third party, making it impossible for the obliged to fulfil the obligation.

## C. Case 3

There is no ground for any action of damages against Y. There is not an agreement on specific behaviour in reaching A's office. X certainly violated a traffic statute, but the statute is not intended to prevent incorrect behaviour in reaching an agreement, instead it is intended to avoid accidents. We must evaluate rules also according to their goals. Hence, the violation of a statute does not make damages to the harmed interest directly

---

18   *See* F.D. Busnelli, *Lesione del credito da parte del terzo* (1964), Milano. For a clear description of jurisprudential evolution on the point *see* F.D. Busnelli, 'La tutela aquiliana del credito: evoluzione giurisprudenziale e significato attuale del principio', in: *Rivista critica del diritto privato* 1988, 288; D. Poletti, 'Dalla lesione del credito alla responsabilitá extracontrattuale da contratto', in: *Contratto Impresa* 1987, 128.

19   In other cases a person is deemed liable when he prevents, by illegal conduct, a party of a contract from performing his obligations. The most common case is that of a wrongdoer (W) who caused an employee (E) personal injuries precluding him from performing his work duties. W is liable for all damages occasioned to E's employer such as extra costs for substituting for E or payments due to E even if impaired. *See*, among others, Tribunale Pavia, 20 novembre 1980, in: *Responsabilitá civile e previdenza* 1981, 236 (nota); Corte Appello Milano, 22 marzo 1982, in: Orient. giur. lav. 1982, 1003; Tribunale Pavia, 28 novembre 1980, in: *Giurisprudenza di merito* 1982, 312; Tribunale Reggio Emilia, 12 ottobre 1943, in: *Archivio circolazione stradale* 1994, 865. For a general introduction *see* F. Ziccardi, *L'induzione all'inadempimento* (1979), Milano, p.271 ff.

20   *See* the introductory remarks on the wrongfulness requirement.

wrongful.[21] Both interests should be jointly considered in the wrongfulness judgement. Consequently, X's violation is irrelevant regarding X–Y relationship. He did not violate any legally protected interest. There is no way to tinge X's conduct with wrongfulness as might have been the case in the hairdresser hypothetical.

## D. Case 4

The violation of Arcadia's ban on oil supplies to Ruritania does not constitute by itself an act of unfair competition. In fact, violation of criminal or administrative laws does not make an action automatically an infraction of Art. 2598 c.c. It can be qualified professionally incorrect if it is used as a means to an end in order to modify the arena of competition.[22] Criminal/administrative wrongs must offend competitors with unjust means to constitute an unfair competition tort according to the quoted rule. The mere fact that D is gaining revenues by violating a law does not make him liable for P's loss of revenue due to the continuance of the rebellion. It is too distant a damage in order to establish a legally significant causal link between such damages and D's illegal conduct. D's violation of the ban is merely an occasion of P's loss of revenues. In fact, even assuming that P would have been the oil supplier during the six-month rebellion period, his loss of revenue is connected to the civil war status and D's illegal conduct is just a factor in its continuance.

## E. Case 5

According to what we said in Case 1, D's conduct can be deemed a violation of Article 2598 c.c. Hence, P could claim damages. However, this is not a clear solution. Two other lines of reasoning could help to sustain the liability hypothesis. P certainly lost a chance to win the competition and, even though losses of chance are not redressable by themselves in our legal system, it could contribute to tinge with wrongfulness (as for civil liability) D's conduct. Moreover, liability might follow directly from the misleading information D gave to the Minister.

We can classify information (that causes damages) into three categories: information as (a) friendly advice; (b) service from a qualified person; (c) as part of a product.

In the first case there is clearly no liability;[23] it is just bad advice. On the contrary, (c) always seems to configure liability of the information supplier. Though there is not a clear line of decisions on the point; prominent scholars consider applicable product liability principles (DPR 24 maggio 1988, n. 224) to (c).[24]

---

21  *See* F.D. Busnelli, 'Illecito civile', in: *Enciclopedia Giuridica Treccani* (1991), Roma, p.16.
22  Corte di Cassazione 1970, n. 914 e Corte di Cassazione 1978, n. 2220.
23  Corte di Cassazione Firenze, 6 dicembre 1915, in: *Rivista di diritto Commerciale* 1916, II, 261 with comments by Mossa, 'La responsabilitá del mandatario per consiglio'.
24  Zoppini, 'Informatizzazione della conoscenza e responsabilitá: i sistemi esperti', in: *Diritto dell'informazione e dell'informatica* 1989, 599, 601-02; Zeno-Zencovich, 'Profili di responsabilitá contrattuale e aquiliana nella fornitura di servizi telematici', in: *Diritto dell'informazione e del l'informatica* 1990, 468 (who doubts products liability are more pro-plaintiff oriented than tradi-

As for hypothetical (b), the closest situation to Case 5, it is the most controversial one. Nevertheless, courts and scholars seem to agree in establishing liability on a person that, due to his special (professional) qualification, with his negligent or careless behaviour creates reliance on the given information.[25] But there are different opinions about the legal criteria to reach this result. Those who think wrongfulness is identified by the violation of an 'absolute' vested right (*diritto soggettivo assoluto*) must select one of the following alternatives: either to deny liability for inexact information due to the absence of a vested right to correct information, or a right to identify 'new' general rights such as a vague 'right to the integrity of one's asset'[26] or a right to 'free choices in contractual activity concerning one's own asset'.[27] Both prongs of the alternative dissatisfy.

Once again the problem is to select interests deserving protection, avoiding, on the one hand, the proliferation of damages requests and, on the other hand, to let deserving interests without protection. Now, we can establish wrongfulness of damages selecting deserving interests according to general principles without the need to qualify them (incorrectly) '*diritti soggettivi*'. As for inexact information, legal principles expressed in article, 1137 and 1338 c.c. and in art. 5 section 1 of DPR 224/1988, might help to qualify wrongful damages those due to non negligent reliance of a foreseeable addressee of an information. In fact, it is possible to find legal criteria fit to delimit the class of a foreseeable addressee worthy of protection.

## F. Case 6

The hypo concerns a topic in which we have to balance contrasting interests such as the right to inform and the right to privacy. After a series of cases, Italian courts reached the conclusion that people do have an 'autonomous right to privacy about their own personal vicissitudes'.[28] However, this right should be balanced with the constitutionally protected right to inform. In order to not incur in slander or defamation, published facts must be true (at least reporters have a duty to check the truth or the verisimilitude of the revealed fact), and their revelation must be in the public interest. The fact that A's

---

[Note 24 continued]
tional tort law); Visintini, *I fatti illeciti, II, La colpa in rapporto agli altri criteri di imputazione della responsabilitá* (1990), Padova, p. 262 (suggests extens a analogy product liability rules to the information field). Troiano, 'Commento all'art. 2', in: Pardolesi and Ponzanelli (eds.), 'Commentario al DPR 24 maggio 1988, n.224', in: *Nuove leggi civile commentate* 1989, 512; Pardolesi and Motti, 'L'idea é mia: lusinghe e misfatti dell'Economics of Information', in: *Diritto dell'informazione e dell'informatica* 1990, 345, express puzzlement on these interpretations.

25   Tribunale Roma, 21 gennaio 1989, n. 669, in: *Temi romana* 1989, II, 85; Appello Roma, 17 ottobre 1989, in: *Giustizia Civile* 1989, I, 2652. In another case a bank was recognized liable. Appello Milano, 14 marzo 1986, *Banca Borsa e titoli di credito* 1987, I, 627.

26   Corte Cassazione, 4 maggio 1982, n. 2765, in: *Giustizia civile* 1982, I, 2739 with comments by Di Majo, 'Ingiustizia del danno e diritti non nominati'; Corte Cassazione, 25 luglio 1987, n.4755, in: *Nuova giurisprudenza civile e commentata* 1987, 386.

27   *See* Luminoso, 'Responsabilitá civile della banca per false o inesatte informazioni', in: *Rivista di diritto commerciale* 1984, I, 197.

28   Corte Cassazione, 27 maggio 1975, n.2129.

previous criminal history was not available from official public records might make its publication a wrong if it does violate some specific rules such as Article 621 of the Italian penal code (Revelation of the content of secret documents).[29] In any event, reporters are not liable for damage to reputation, given the truth of the information and the public considerable interest to know that piece of information. However, according to the principles fixed in Art. 2 of the Constitution, Art. 7 c.c. for the protection of the name may be extended by analogy to the public image of the person. This means that a 'right to personal identity' (that is, the sum of intellectual, political, religious and professional values for which a person is known in a given social context) is identified and protected with injunctory and compensatory relief.[30]

## G. Case 7

The hypo says that D does not give X a defensibly accurate view of P. This can either be (a) a violation of D's personal identity and reputation or (b) an incorrect information. Under (a), if the facts stated are true and relevant in D's judgement as a good employee, it seems he is not violating P's rights but expressing his own opinion of him and after P's own request. Nevertheless, if he is wilfully or negligently exaggerating (even true) facts he is liable for damages.

The hypo (b) suggests information given in the reference are not entirely correct, at least they are biased. Hence, according to what we said under Case 5, D should be liable, given his knowledge for the foreseeable addressee of information and for the foreseeable result of such a description.

## H. Case 8

All the requirements of Article 2043 c.c., seem established in the case. Doubts may exist on the unlawfulness one. Undoubtedly, the innkeeper (O) is causing a personal injury to V. He knows V is almost drunk, since O served him alcoholics, and he should understand that even a slight push is enough to make a drunk person fall. He is negligently violating V's constitutionally protected right to health and his action is both the *de facto* cause and the legal cause of V's damages. However, he thinks he is acting in self-defence. Article 2044 c.c. ('Whoever causes damages in defending himself or others is not liable') would free him entirely from liability if he acted in self-defence.

---

29  The publication of reserved information in the file concerning a divorce trial originated liability for damages. Tribunale Roma, 16 febbraio 1989, in: *Diritto dell'informazione e dell'informatica* 1990, 539, with note of V. Zeno-Zencovich, 'Lesione della riservatezza attraverso la pubblicazione di atti di un procedimento civile'.

30  *See* Tribunale Roma, 15 maggio 1995, in: *Diritto dell' informazione e dell' informatica* 1996, with note by G. Napolitano, 'Il diritto all'oblio esiste (ma non lo si dice)', a case of defamation where a newspaper published an article published thirty years before. Such promotional publication caused damage to the honour of a person who thirty years before was involved in a murder. The damaged person claimed damages because his right to make the public forget his story was unprotected.

Nevertheless the hypo suggests that O acted in putative self-defence and courts might still ask him to indemnify damages.[31] Note that in this case a reduced amount of money (indemnity) determined by the judge is due under criteria of equity according to Art. 2045, by definition it cannot be full compensation.

## I. Case 9

Art. 844 c.c.:

> 'The owner of a land cannot stop the nuisance of smoke, heat, exhalations, noises, jolts, and similar propagation coming from a neighbour's land, if they do not exceed standard tolerability, considering also conditions of the site.

Applying this rule judges must balance production exigencies with landowner interests.'

All six hypos can be solved under Art. 2043 c.c.[32] and Art. 844 c.c.

*(a)  O has a valid permit 'to produce' smell*
In any event A's strong aversion to smell does not prevent O from producing it. If O has a permit for his production, most probably the smell by-product was already considered by it. However, smell cannot be stopped unless it exceeds standard tolerability.[33] Even if the latter is the case, judicial authority may still let production exigencies to prevail.[34]

Headache constantly caused by persistent smell is an objective pathology leading to personal injury (damage to health – *danno alla salute*). Expressly it is damage to B's health deserving compensation under general principles of tort law regardless of valid permits for O's production activity. Courts clearly say that nuisances are never tolerable under Article 844 when there is damage to human health.[35]

Diminished value of the land, considering the original use and ways of enjoying it, is a compensable damage if demonstrated.[36] Note, however, that judges evaluating tolerability and choosing to use injunctive and/or compensatory relief may decide to award an indemnity to C, letting O produce smell.

*(b)  O does not have a valid permit 'to produce' smell*
*See* above a.A.

---

31  *See* Tribunale Arezzo, 16 marzo 1960, in: *Foro italiano* 1960, I, 858.
32  *See supra*, note 3.
33  In cases of this type there could be a liability on basis of Environmental Law n. 349/1986, art. 18. But this law does not allow a person to claim damages. Instead, this law protects the state and public organizations against environmental damages.
34  For a similar case *see* Corte di Cassazione, Sezioni Unite, 19 luglio 1985, n. 4263, as quoted by Busnelli, 'Danno alla salute e danno ambientale come sciogliere il "nodo gordiano"?', in: *Rivista Italiana di Medicina Legale* 1993, 287, 290.
35  *See*, for example, Corte di Cassazione, 14 dicembre 1968, n. 3971.
36  Corte di Cassazione, 13 gennaio 1975, n.111, in: *Foro italiano* 1975, I, 2223.

*See* above a.B. In any event B can seek injunctive relief in order to stop immediately the smell. Judges may impose on O the alternative of either stopping his production or taking all the necessary steps to prevent nasty smells.

*See* above a.C.

## J. Case 10

(a)  D is neither causing any personal injury to the blind person nor does he have any specific duty to avoid him damages. Otherwise Article 2043 c.c. wrongfulness requirement would be easily established. Hence, under our laws D is not liable, even though Article 593 section 2 of the Italian penal code (c.p.) punishes whoever, 'finding [...], a person injured or otherwise in peril, fails to give him needed assistance or to immediately inform the authorities'.[37] Also under this rule we need to find a duty to prevent damages rooted in a contractual assumption of it or in special relationships such as between parents and children, teachers and pupils. In fact, *neminem laedere* principle does not imply a general duty to act in protection of a third party we did not put in danger.[38]

Putting aside this negative solution imposed by Italian law in action, we would express some reflections we deem useful in the construction of European principles of tort law.

Unless we identify wrongfulness with the violation of vested rights or, anyway, well-defined protected spheres we must find some criteria to be given to judges in selecting interest deserving civil liability protection (i.e., compensation). Koziol suggests several elements to be considered in order to establish wrongfulness. However, we still lack some criteria to weigh them. Now take for example our heartless person in Case 10a. Under most of our laws he is not liable: he owes no duty to prevent 'blind people to fall in perilous holes'. No prescription of law asks him to behave as a good Samaritan even though he has virtually no costs in doing so. He does not incur in civil or criminal sanction even if a shout would have prevented serious personal injuries. Nevertheless, if we read, say, Article 593 section 2 c.p. and Article 2043 c.c. with the glasses of our Constitution imbued with solidarity principles, we might tinge with unlawfulness D's conduct establishing wrongfulness of the damages at least in this case. This solution is far to become law in action. However, we think it is a good example of how the European research group we are building up might work out clear legal principles of tort law availing ourselves also of our common constitutional principles. In fact, our legal traditions and moreover our constitutional principles emanate from the same cultural background of freedom and spirit of justice.

(b)  Also under this hypo, D is liable if he had a duty to prevent damages to others. His duty derives from his lawful activity of digging a hole in the public road. The created risk imposed on him the duty adequately to fence the hole and to take  adequate steps to

---

37   Moreover, penalty is incremented if from this failure to rescue derives a personal injury and doubled if the injured person dies.

38   Corte di Cassazione, 9 gennaio 1979, n. 116.

repair the barrier, once informed of the vandalous acts. D's conduct is unlawful and he is liable for damages according to the general rule of Article 2043 c.c. unless no possible or due step could be taken. Moreover Article 2050 c.c. regulates civil liability for dangerous activities: 'Anyone who damages others carrying out a dangerous activity, by its nature or by the nature of the used means, should redress them [damages], unless he proves he adopted all due measures to avoid damage.' It is not clear if we can plainly hold D's activity dangerous in the sense of Art. 2050 c.c.[39] even though there are several prescriptions of law to protect public safety in digging holes in public roads. In case of an affirmative answer there would be an inversion of the burden of proof, making it easier for the damaged person to find compensation.

(c) Given the hypothetical, the doctor is clearly liable. He certainly is violating Article 593 section 2 c.p. and the damages he caused are unlawful. Moreover, the new Code of Medical Ethics expressly provides for medical doctors a duty to help in such occasions (Art. 7).[40]

---

39 As it would be in the case of underground excavation in the city. *See* Tribunale Palermo, 23 gennaio 1992, in: *Rassegna giuridica energia elettrica* 1993, 217.
40 The Italian Code of Medical Ethics has not a direct legal power but it is useful in order to give a specification to the rule of diligence codified by Art. 1176 c.c.

# Some Remarks on the Borderline Between Contract and Tort Liability

## Francesco D. Busnelli and Giovanni Comandé

First of all we should ask a preliminary question: is there any room to overcome the sharp alternative between contract and tort? Better way: is there a unavoidable alternative or can they be interpreted as two different techniques of protection for deserving interests to be used according to circumstances?

It is a pretty common understanding that their common frontiers are mobile. Often, interpretations move toward the expansion of one at the expenses of the other, but the pendulum seems often to oscillate from one to the other regardless of real differences in their structure.

Among Italian scholars there are two main trends, at least, on the borderline between contract and tort.

Several scholars think that, according to Italian law, liability protection in contractual relationships is stronger than the tort one because the damaged party need not establish fault of the debtor: it comes as easily as directly from the breach (non-fulfilment or misfeasance). Nevertheless, this does not mean that fault is not relevant in evaluating breach of contract. In fact, the conduct of both creditor and debtor must be evaluated under the fault principle as a standard of care. Moreover the proof of fault may not play such a burdening role even in liability rules grounded on the fault principle.

The presumed better protection provided by contract, joined with the concept of tort as a set of typical hypotheses that need the violation of a perfect right for establishing liability, grounds the first trend. In many legal systems a rule of liability for non-fulfilment (or incorrect fulfilment) is established parallel to tort liability in several areas, such as medical malpractice or contract regarding the transportation of people. Often the implementation of the so called '*obligation de sécurité*' (see the French experience) or 'duties of protection' (see, e.g., the German experience) is used to expand the scope of contract. This is true especially when physical integrity or credits (chose in action) are at stake.

In the end, the result of this line of reasoning is to reduce the relevance of tort law via an expansion of contract. However, this solution apparently leaves without protection damages that do not affect perfect rights and are hardly brought under a valid contract. These losses are often called pure economic losses.

83

*H. Koziol (ed.), Unification of Tort Law: Wrongfulness, 83–86.*
©1998 *Kluwer Law International. Printed in The Netherlands.*

Often the need to resort to contract is imposed by a theory of tort based on hypothesis thought to be fixed and typified once forever. In Italy this concept was connected to the will to constrain the wide formula of Art. 2043 c.c. to the violation of perfect rights. This because of the fear of an extension of liability without limits. Anyway, floodgates arguments can appear in every legal system. Moreover comparison teaches us that legal systems considering general rules of tort law with broad description (so called non-typified systems such as French based on Art. 1382 of the *code civil* and Italy based on Art. 2043 civil code) adopted restrictive interpretation of the rule to restate the formula and countries with a closed list of torts embraced line of reasoning leading to the expansion of one of more tort (see, for example, the expansion of the tort of negligence in the common law area or in the Germany experience). Hence, the preconceived election of a typical system or of an atypical one is misleading.

Note that in Italy infringement of a so-called absolute right is no longer needed to gain tort protection.

A second trend tries to reduce differences between tort and contractual liability, looking to their common grounds.

The history of tort and contract liability can be written as the history of two different remedies/answers to the same question: wrongfulness of damage.

Both of these primarily rest on fault and wrongfulness ('*ingiustizia del danno*') of damages is required. In fact, a problem of wrongfulness arises as well for contractual obligations, apart from the fact that wrongfulness is expressly mentioned only in Article 2043 c.c. Non-fulfilment poses the problem, at least, for the qualification of the interests regulated with the contract. Interests usually protected under tort principles can be poured by the parties under contract law. It is the case, for example, of the interest to physical integrity internalized in the duty to transport 'safely' a person in the contract of carriage regulated by Art. 1681 c.c.

The borderlines between tort and contract are certainly mobile, and most of the classical criteria for distinguishing between them seem to lose strength. However, the basic logic that differentiates them still rests on the existence of a primary obligation that is not satisfied (contractual responsibility) or upon its non-existence (tort).

In any event, the choice between the two liability rules is somehow more a matter of strategy than it can seem at first glance. When a relationship can easily be established and contracts are a firm source of obligations there are no reasons to avoid the contractual liability instrument: parties' regulation will govern. Note, however, that the law can limit parties' freedom of choice according to the importance of the interest (say, for example, health) not allowing them to regulate it freely.

In the same way, there is no reason to fear tort liability, if no contractual relationship can be established without the use of abnormal artifices and interests worthy of protection claim its protection. Using the wrongfulness requirement it is possible to extend tort liability without reaching an unacceptable bystander liability rule or recurring to a fake creation of 'new' (absolute) rights every time an interest is deemed worthy of protection. In fact, it is enough to 'verify, through the wrongfulness of damage requirement, the existence of damage to interest worthy of being compensated, in that they are juridically important according to the rules and principles of the legal system.'

Moreover, causes of action for tort and contract liability might well concur.

Preferring tort liability under the above conditions would ease the solution of several practical matters, but it would not mean the obliteration of contract. For example, Cases 11 and 12 of the wrongfulness hypothetical would be easily solved under contract law. In both cases breach of contract is certainly at stake. However, if the contract is not agreed upon or it is void, we neither need to hypothesize a 'contractual' duty to inform (about the sore spot or the characteristics of the computer) nor a right to the free exercise of one's own freedom of contract, infringed by the illicit withdrawal of information, to establish liability under either contract or tort law. Italian law (Art. 1337 c.c.) gives a specific solution requiring parties to behave with correctness and good faith during negotiation. These principles set forth the legal criteria on which selecting interests deserving legal protection and (in)correct behaviours we should deter. The problem of qualifying the liability (as contractual or tortious) would not even remain in abstract.

Hence, the alternative between the expansion of contract at the expense of tort and vice versa seems to be a false alternative once we understand their common grounds and their way of operation.

The proposed key for interpretation looks for homogeneous legal principles in different areas upon which to qualify the worthiness of interests at stake and consequently to establish the wrongfulness of their violation.

We think it is possible to work out a clear-cut criterion of wrongfulness to be used either in tort or in contract. This is one of the most ambitious challenges of our common project.

However, borderlines and differences between contract and tort still remain. Those liability régimes were usually distinguished just by those variances in their disciplines. Nowadays, those distinctions are not as clear cut as they were in the past, but a short list of them might help.[1]

The basic distinction between tort and contract responsibility rests on the existence of an (unsatisfied) primary obligation for contractual responsibility and upon its non-existence for tort.

As we said above, today infringement by a third party of a right to the performance of a given obligation leads to (tort) liability.

Likewise a clear distinction cannot be drawn upon the assumption that contract responsibility presumes fault.

Clauses limiting liability were deemed automatically in violation of public order (policy), hence void. On the contrary they are permissible under contract law, unless they are against public order (policy) or limit liability for gross negligence and malice. Nowadays liability limitation clauses for special rules of liability are not by definition void.

It is commonly said that tort awards also unforeseeable damages while contract would authorize only those foreseeable damages at the time of the agreement. However, Italian judges sometimes tend not to award unforeseeable damages under tort law saying

---

1    An updated and convincing analysis was recently made by F. Giardina, *Responsabilità contrattuale e responsabilità extracontrattuale* (1993), Milano, from which we used the list in the text.

the event itself was not foreseeable hence it was out of the sphere of the tortfeasor (it is often the case under decisions about liability under Art. 2051 and 2052 c.c.). Moreover the rule under contract law has several exceptions (see Art. 1225 c.c.).

Different time limitations still exist (ten years for breach of contract and 5 years for tort compensation: see Art. 2946–2947 c.c.). Nevertheless concurrence of both causes of action enervates any clear cut distinction.

On the contrary there is no reason to sustain that moral damages (*pretium doloris*) can be redressed only under tort law. It was said that tort law covers an area better suited to receive criminal sanction. Hence, since Art. 2059 c.c. establishes that moral damage can be redressed only when prescribed by the law and the main rule is Article 185 of the penal code, there was a trend to exclude moral damages for breach of contract. Nevertheless, even under a literal interpretation of Art. 2059 there is not any ground to exclude compensation for *pretium doloris* also under contract.

# The Netherlands

WRONGFULNESS IN THE DUTCH CONTEXT

Jaap Spier

## I. Introduction

At first glance, art. 6:162 BW seems to provide a comprehensive answer to the question posed. It reads:

> '1. A person who commits an unlawful act toward another which can be imputed to him, must repair the damage the other person suffers as a consequence thereof.
> 2. Except where there is a ground of justification, the following acts are deemed to be unlawful: violation of a right, an act or omission violating a statutory duty or a rule of unwritten law pertaining to proper social conduct.
> 3. An unlawful act can be imputed to its author if it results from his fault or from a cause for which he is answerable according to law or common opinion.'

Moreover, art. 6:163 further restricts the scope of liability:

> 'There is no obligation to repair damage when the violated norm does not have as its purpose the protection from damage such as that suffered by the victim.'

However, appearances are deceptive. There has already for decades been a fierce legal controversy about the exact meaning of the fundamentals of tort law and the way they should be applied. Be it that in the overwhelming majority of cases the importance of this controversy is rather remote. And, perhaps more amazingly, neither courts nor practioners seem to care.

*H. Koziol (ed.), Unification of Tort Law: Wrongfulness, 87–100.*
©1998 *Kluwer Law International. Printed in The Netherlands.*

## II. The Requirement of '*onrechtmatigheid*' (art. 6:162 para. 2)

Violation of a rule of unwritten law clearly calls for *ad hoc* decisions. However, to some extent its meaning can be clarified in specific areas by phrasing sub-rules. See Section VI below. In quite a number of cases Courts do not explain why the act at stake is a tort or not. It is often the case of a magic word.

Violation of a statutory duty has to be understood in a broad sense. It covers legislation enacted by the State of the Netherlands as well as by local government, and also violation of permits granted by public authorities.

Infringement of a right covers personal injury (defamation included) and damage to goods or financial interests.[1]

It is open to debate whether *mere violation* of a statutory duty or of a right constitutes unlawfulness (in the sense of *onrechtmatigheid*). This can be demonstrated by the following examples:

I.   Car A and car B collide. It could be argued that A violated B's right and vice versa.
II.  Factory A is connected to the public sewer system; A is entitled (by permit) to a discharge of 1000 litres a day. A only needs to discharge 600. A's neighbour, factory B, is not connected to the public sewer. It produces 300 litres of effluent a day. A and B agree that the latter is allowed to do so via A's connexion. Without informing A, B increases its effluent level by 200%. From then on, the combined discharge causes damage to the sewerage system. B is not worth suing. A clearly violated the terms of the permit, although he cannot be blamed at all. It not necessarily reasonable to hold him liable for the *mere reason* that he violated a statutory duty.[2]
III. During a housewarming party organised by A, his guest B upsets a glass of red wine, which damages A's carpet. Should this mere fact be sufficient to constitute unlawfulness?[3]

## III. Fault (*Schuld*)

Art. 6:162 para. 3 requires that the act can be imputed to the tortfeasor. Either because he is at fault or because his act (or omission) can be imputed to him according to law or common opinion.

The legislator apparently had in mind that para. 3 would play a useful role in keeping liability within reasonable limits. However, it is very much open to debate whether it is of much use. The proof of the pudding is in the eating: in which cases can the defendant successfully argue that he was not at fault?

---

1   *See* Asser-Hartkamp III, No. 34 ff.
2   These are the facts of a case, decided by the Supreme Court (HR 20-4-1990, NJ 1991,53). The question addressed in the text was not at stake (surprisingly enough).
3   This example is borrowed from H.L.J. Roelvink (Vice-President of the Supreme Court), CJHB-bundel, p. 325 ff. Roelvink also touches upon the controversy mentioned in the text.

Some commentators subscribe to the doctrinal view – which is along the lines of what the legislator had in mind – that the difference between unlawfulness (para. 2) and fault (*schuld*, para. 3) is the following. The former addresses the *act* (is it allowed), the latter the *tortfeasor* (can he be blamed).[4] In this view, it can easily be explained why a three-year-old child, burning down a house, was not liable under the Old Civil Code. The *act* clearly was unlawful, but the child cannot be blamed (did not have '*schuld*'). In normal cases, the difference is not utterly useful. If the act is unlawful, the tortfeasor will almost always be at fault.

The above implies that under the Old Civil Code the answer was clear: minors below a certain age and severely mentally handicapped persons could invoke a defence: the act can not be imputed, due to lack of fault.[5] Apart from those cases, examples were very rare indeed, with the exception of a few cases of mistake of law or facts.[6] The former two no longer play a role. Children below the age of 14 are not liable in tort (art. 6:164); mental or physical handicap can no longer be invoked by the defendant (art. 6:165 para. 1).[7]

As set out in para. 2, '*schuld*' is not a requirement *per se* (it can be substituted by a cause for which he is answerable according to law or common opinion). As an example: public authorities are liable for damage, suffered due to annulment of, e.g., a permit granted by them. Even if, at the time of granting the permit, they had no reason to reckon with that possibility, because the permit was in compliance with the law as it stood at that time. Under those circumstances, it can hardly be argued that the public authority was at fault. Still, it is liable because its act has to be imputed to it.[8]

Apart from the above differences between the old and the present Civil Code, the legislator did not aim to change the system materially. It follows from this that art. 6:162 para 3 is somewhat useless. At least: if we approach the issue along the lines just described. Some commentators believe that it nevertheless is of importance, because it requires (a kind of) negligence (in the sense of para. 2: a violation of a rule of proper social conduct).[9] Given that interpretation it is (more or less) a duplication of the third category of para. 2. The consequence thereof is that it becomes an additional requirement if a claim is based on one of the first two categories of para. 2. That assumption could justify why B is not liable in the cases mentioned *supra* in Section II.

## IV. How should we Interpret art. 6:162 paras. 2 and 3?

The more predominant view seems to be that the facts of the cases mentioned *supra* Section II are *in themselves* insufficient to establish A's liability. But there is still

---

4   *See* also for more details, Asser-Hartkamp III, No. 70 ff.
5   *See* for details *Onrechtmatige Daad* IG (Jansen), No. 247.
6   *Ibid.*, No. 258 ff.
7   At least in relation to 'acts'.
8   HR 30.1.1987, NJ 1988, 70 MS.
9   *See* for details *Onrechtmatige Daad*, art. 162, lid 2, aant. 3 and 72.

disagreement about the question as to *why* he is not liable.[10] Some authors believe that violation of a right[11] or of a statutory duty is not unlawful, unless it is also in conflict with a rule of unwritten law pertaining to proper social conduct. Others are of the opinion that A is not liable, unless his act can be imputed to him. In the latter approach art. 6:162 para. 3 has to be understood as: the conduct at stake is also in violation of a rule of unwritten law, pertaining to proper social conduct. In their view, para. 3 has the meaning set out at the end of Section III *supra*. The Supreme Court never explicitly addressed the question. Some judgments could be interpreted to adhere the former, some to be based on the latter view.

For practical purposes this doctrinal fight is not of much importance. It has hardly ever played a role in real life. Dutch lawyers are not fond of legal doctrine, nor is the Supreme Court.[12] Be that as it may, for the purpose of drafting European principles of tort law the Dutch experience – or to be more precise: its confusion – might be interesting. It shows that such a system can hardly serve as a model for Europe!

## V. The Duty of Care

The duty of care (*Schutznorm*) has long been a rather obsolete criterion.[13] Times change; so do torts. Suing attorneys, notaries public, auditors and the like has become popular. As a matter of fact, plaintiffs will often be their contractual counterparts. In those cases tort law plays no role whatsoever. Third parties may also suffer damage from their acts. Under Dutch law they have to base their claims on tort law. Although case law is far from abundant, it seems likely that it boils down to the question of whether the defendant knew or should have known that the third 'party' would rely on its acts or could suffer damage in consequence thereof.[14]

Apart from these topics, the duty of care is of rather limited importance.[15]

One should bear in mind that causation often is very much related to the duty of care phenomenon. It actually plays a role in dismissing claims by 'third parties' suffering

---

10   *See*, for details J. Spier, *Schoordijkbundel*, p. 267 ff. and *preadvies Nederlandse Juristen-Vereniging 1996*, pp. 250–251.

11   Another approach – which boils down to the same thing – is to hold that the act cannot be considered as a violation of a right, e.g., because it is of insufficient importance. *See* Asser-Hartkamp III, No. 37 ff.

12   One should bear in mind that it has to limit itself to the legal arguments put forward.

13   I leave aside whether it still plays a role or whether it has 'merged' with unlawfulness (art. 6:162 para 2). *See* HR 30-9-1994, NJ 1996, 196 and J. Spier, WPNR 6168, pp. 109–110.

14   *See* A.T. Bolt, *preadvies Nederlandse Juristen-Vereniging 1996*, p. 152 ff. and *Onrechtmatige Daad* III.VI (Hartlief and Tjittes).

15   *See* for a complete overview *Onrechtmatige Daad*, art. 163 (Van Maanen). There was an upsurge in connection with the cleaning by the Dutch State of soil polluted by X and owned by Y. The question arose whether wrongful pollution was a tort against the State. This topic was heavily debated; the Supreme Court delivered various most interesting judgments on this topic. Yet it can be disregarded because recent legislation provides the State with remedy against X.

damage due to unlawful disruption of gas pipes and electricity cables.[16] Yet, for rather mysterious reasons, case law and doctrine do not seem to care whether such cases should be perceived from the angle of duty of care or causation.[17]

## VI. Capita Selecta

### A. *Increased Danger*

Increased danger is a well-known source of damage. Whether it constitutes a tort depends on: the likelihood of damage, the nature and size of the damage incurred and the cost of precautionary measures.[18] Case law shows a clear trend in establishing liability in the case of personal injury, even if the likelihood was rather remote, unless the defendant is a private person not acting in the course of a business or profession.[19]

### B. *Professional Liability*

The yardstick is a reasonably capable and reasonably acting professional.[20,21] Case law on liability outside the scope of a contractual relationship is scarce. If we focus on jurisprudence about professional liability in the contractual setting, it appears that it is not very consistent. The Supreme Court delivered some rather demanding judgments;[22] generally speaking, the yardstick is quite fair and the outcome of cases far from surprising (seen from a Dutch perspective). Case law is less reluctant to establish liability if medical malpractice is at stake, probably because it is about personal injury.

---

16   Even though factories, suffering damage because the supply was cut off, are entitled to compensation. Difficulties arise in connection with claims by companies depending on these factories and even more so in relationship to claims by suppliers of the latter. *See* for more details my observations on the relevant hypothetical and *preadvies Nederlandse Juristen-Vereniging 1996*, p. 312 ff.

17   The duty of care approach was followed in HR 14-3-1958, NJ 1961, 570.

18   HR 5-11-1965, NJ 1966, 139 GJS. *See*, for many details C.C. van Dam, *Zorgvuldigheidsnorm en aansprakelijkheid*; A.T. Bolt, *op. cit.*, p. 160 ff.

19   *See*, for details A.T. Bolt, *op. cit.*, p.180 ff. and J. Spier, *op. cit*,. p. 318 ff. The Supreme Court was also rather lenient for a defendant, clearly acting in the course of his business, in: HR 31-3-1995, NJ 1997, 592 CJHB. This judgment, which met fierce criticism, seems an exception. *See* Case 8 below.

20   At least, in a contractual setting. HR 19-4-1996, NJ 1996, 727 WMK (about liability of a receiver) seems to suggest that it could be slightly different to the detriment of third 'parties', in that the Court would be more reluctant to establish liability. I tend to believe that the difference would be rather marginal.

21   *See*, for details A.T. Bolt, *op. cit.*, p. 118 ff.

22   *See* also A.T. Bolt, *op. cit.*, pp 158–159.

## C. Economic Torts

It is impossible to describe this *'mer à boire'* in a few words.[23] To put it briefly: case law is apparently inspired by the *laissez faire* principle, rather to the benefit of defendants.

Mere taking advantage of a third 'party's' non-compliance with its contractual obligations does not give rise to liability in tort.[24] Liability could be established by additional circumstances such as acting with intent or by doing so frequently; in addition, serious harm suffered by the other 'party' is required.[25]

Making profit out of the know-how or goodwill of an employee formerly employed by a competitor does not give rise to a claim.[26] Calling for a boycott is not a tort *per se*; additional circumstances like disproportionate damage, can make it a tort.[27]

## D. Defamation

Defamation does not *per se* establish liability. As a general rule, it does if the tortfeasor knows his statement to be incorrect. If it is not – or the tortfeasor had reason to believe it is not – it depends on various circumstances whether the 'injured' has a valid claim. The interests of the 'parties' will be weighed.

The issue mainly arises in the context of statements in the press, via radio or television. It is often claimed by the defendant that they serve the general interest. Whether this defence will be honoured, depends on the nature of the statements (often suspicions), the consequences for the victim, and the gravity of the suspicions or the abuse seen from the perspective of the general interest,[28] whether the statements are based on evidence and the wording and presentation thereof. The issue has to be considered in the light of Art. 10 ECHR.[29] It would be a mistake to assume that the freedom of expression necessarily prevails.[30]

Mere opinions (even conceited) or qualifications will rarely be actionable.[31]

## E. Product Liability

Damage caused by defective products is covered by the Dutch implementation of the EC directive if personal injury or damage suffered by a 'consumer' over a certain amount are concerned. In this respect, the law has already been harmonized. Curiously enough,

---

23  Misleading publicity will be disregarded; it is covered by specific articles (6:194 f. BW).
24  *See* for details *Onrechtmatige Daad* III (Van Maanen), No. 29 ff.
25  *See* for further elaboration *Onrechtmatige Daad* VI (Martens), No. 81.
26  *Onrechtmatige Daad* VI (Martens), No. 74.3.
27  *Onrechtmatige Daad* VI (Martens), No. 96/97.
28  Even serious suspicions may be(come) relatively unimportant, e.g., whether or not a person committed a serious crime decades ago. In this connection, it is probably relevant whether it is about, e.g., a politician or an 'average Dutchman'.
29  *See* for elaboration HR 6-1-1995, NJ 1995, 422 EJD.
30  HR 21-1-1994, NJ 1994, 473 DWFV. *See* for an instructive case also ECHR 26-4-1995, Publ. ECHR, Series A, vol. 313.
31  *See*, for details Asser-Hartkamp III, No. 237 ff.

case law and doctrine are rare with regard to the remaining cases. Consequently, it is difficult to give an outline of Dutch law in this respect.[32]

We may take it that the mere fact that a product appears to be defective is insufficient. Negligence of the manufacturer either in compounding the product or in the (control of) the production process is required. As to the question whether or not a product is 'defective', the criterion of the directive applies as well. The manufacturer will have to explain (i.e.: not to prove) why he was not at fault.[33] Attribution of specific qualities, which the product does not have, in advertising will equally lead to liability.[34]

## F. Abus de Droit

Art. 3:13 para 2 BW reads:

> 'Instances of abuse of right are the exercise of a right with the sole intention of harming another or for a purpose other than that for which it was granted; or the exercise of a right where its holder could not reasonably have decided to exercise it, given the disproportion between the interest to exercise the right and the harm caused thereby.'

The predominant view is that abuse of right has to be regarded as a tort.[35]

## G. Labour Accidents

Art. 7:658 BW[36] deals with liability for labour accidents and occupational diseases. It comes close to a strict liability. For that reason, I will leave it aside.

## H. Nuisance (Noise, Stench and the Like)

Art. 5:37 BW provides a rather useless rule about liability for nuisance such as offensive smells, noise and the like:

> 'A landowner may not cause nuisance to owners of other properties to a degree or in a fashion which is unlawful according to article 162 of Book 6, for example by the emanation of noise, vibrations, foul odours, smoke or gas, or by depriving other owners of light, air or support.'

It follows from this article that the question whether the plaintiff has a course of action depends on art. 6:162 BW, quoted in the Introduction to this article.

---

32    *See* J. Spier, *preadvies Nederlandse Juristen-Vereniging 1996*, p. 234 ff.
33    HR 6.12.1996, NJ 1997, 219.
34    *See* for details *Onrechtmatige Daad* VIII (Michiels van Kessenich-Hoogendam), No. 183 ff.
35    Asser-Hartkamp III, No. 56. *See* for a slightly different view *Vermogensrecht*, art. 13 (Den Tonkelaar), aant. 31.
36    Which came into force on 1 January 1997.

Here, too, courts are rather unresponsive in establishing liability. This is apparently because nuisance can hardly be avoided in our modern society.[37] Whether a tort is committed depends on factors like the degree of noise etc.,[38] the frequency, the degree of the inconvenience and the damage[39] caused to the plaintiff, the cost of precautionary measures,[40] local circumstances,[41] whether the plaintiff settled at the spot before or after the activities started[42] and the interest served by the activities causing the nuisance.[43]

## VII. The Importance of Various Factors and their Interrelationship

It follows from the above that the greater part of the factors, mentioned, play a role. Doctrine nor courts are very explicit about their relative relevance. With this disclaimer, I will try to elaborate on this topic:

*1.*    There seems to be a clear trend to establish liability in case of personal injury. This policy argument is explicitly revealed in case law about traffic accidents,[44] product liability[45] and labour accidents.[46] The predominant view is, I think, that the same is true in other areas. But there are exceptions to this rule. As already pointed out above, courts are reluctant in relation to nuisance. Although it is a (slightly) different topic, they are also reluctant in relation to the consequences of unjustified imprisonment, press statements by prosecution officers about suspected persons and more generally correct but defaming publications which can well have a tremendous impact on personal life.

Generally speaking, courts are more reluctant in relation to damage to property and even more so as regards pure economic loss. Again, the law is not entirely consistent. Damage suffered as a consequence of a decision by public authorities (like a permit) which is annulled by the competent Court will be actionable, irrespective whether or not the authority can be blamed; despite the fact that the damage will often be just pure economic loss.

*2.*    It is difficult to say whether or not insurance coverage (either by the plaintiff or the defendant) or insurability play a role. I tend to answer the question in the affirmative,

---

37    J. Spier, *preadvies Nederlandse Juristen-Vereniging 1996*, pp. 309–310.
38    HR 10-3-1972, NJ 1972, 278 GJS.
39    For the latter, *see*: HR 28-4-1995, NJ 1995, 513.
40    HR 9-1-1981, NJ 1981, 227 CJHB.
41    HR 3-5-1991, NJ 1991, 476.
42    HR 24-11-1995, NJ 1996, 164.
43    HR 15-2-1991, NJ 1992, 639 CJHB.
44    In relation to pedestrians and bicyclists. *See* for details J. Spier, *preadvies Nederlandse Juristen-Vereniging 1996*, p. 207 ff.
45    And the DES case about joint and several liability; *see The Limits of Liability* (1996), pp. 123–124.
46    The same is true for the consequences of contributory negligence of children in the context of increased danger, e.g., HR 8-12-1989, NJ 1990, 778 CJHB.

especially in relation to personal injury.[47] Yet, it is impossible to prove this statement. The Supreme Court referred to mandatory insurance of car drivers in a number of decisions; it was used as an argument to justify rather far reaching[48] liability rules. Apart from cases about traffic accidents, the Court does not openly rely on or refer to the issue.[49]

I should not be surprised if the Courts might be(come) more reluctant as from the very moment that it might appear that insurability could vanish into thin air. We may take it for granted that this will only happen in connection with specific categories of liability.

*3.* Foreseeability plays a prominent role. A high degree of probability that damage could occur will soon constitute a tort. This does not mean that foreseeability is the dominant factor. Noise, for example, will often cause irritation and equally well may have financial repercussions, e.g., on the prices of houses (factories, airports etc.). Nevertheless, the 'injured' will certainly face serious difficulties in getting compensation. See *supra* and Case 9.

The chance that a car accident on a highway will cause traffic jams is quite considerable. Still, those who suffer damage in consequence thereof will have no chance to sue the tortfeasor.[50]

*4.* The size of the damage will probably not be an argument. Dutch law provides quite some possibilities to keep liability within reasonable limits.[51]

*5.* The cost of taking precautionary measures can play a role, especially if they would be disproportionate. Oddly enough, this also goes for the employer's liability for labour accidents.[52] In other words: the mere fact that personal injury is at stake is not *necessarily* decisive.

# VIII. Strict Liability

The Dutch Civil Code establishes strict liability for damage, suffered as a consequence of:
– defective goods (art. 6:173 BW);
– defective premises and roads (art. 6:174 BW);
– dangerous substances (art. 6:175 BW);
– dumping sites (art. 6:176 BW);
– bore-holes (art. 6:177 BW);

---

47  *See* for a similar view, with further details, T. Hartlief and R.P.J.L. Tjittes, *Verzekeringen en aansprakelijkheid*, especially pp. 1–2 and p. 15 ff.
48  Not far-reaching in itself, but seen from the perspective of the relevant legislation. *See* J. Spier, *preadvies Nederlandse Juristen-Vereniging 1996*, p. 227 ff.
49  With one exception in a contractual setting (HR 5-1-1968, NJ 1968, 102 GJS).
50  *See* for details my observations in: Spier (ed.), *The Limits of Expanding Liability* (1998), p. 162 ff..
51  *See* for details my contribution in: Spier (ed.), *The Limits of Liability* (1996), p. 93 ff.
52  HR 6-4-1990, NJ 1990, 573 PAS.

–  animals (art. 6:179);
–  defective products (art. 6:185 ff = implementation of EC directive)

Neither unlawfulness nor fault are required. I shall leave aside whether the same is true of the duty of care (Schutznorm); the question seems fairly academic.[53]

## IX. The Cases

### A. Case 1

Selling at lower prices than competitors is not a tort. Opinions are devided as to whether the same is true for dumping with the purpose to eliminate competitors.[54] Be that as it may, I hardly doubt that D's act is actionable in the given circumstances. His only purpose is to cut out P, without any interest for himself. See *supra*, *abus de droit*.

### B. Case 2

D will be liable, because provoking non-compliance with a contract is a violation of a rule of unwritten law; the conduct is in conflict with proper social conduct. Probably *per se*, but certainly if it aims to enrich oneself.[55]

### C. Case 3

The mere fact that Y violates a traffic statute is insufficient. X can probably only sue Y if Y's conduct violates a rule of unwritten law pertaining to proper social conduct.[56] I doubt whether that is the case.

Even assuming that the answer might be in the affirmative, X will have to clear the hurdle of duty of care. The traffic statute clearly does not aim to protect X from the damage that he suffered. Needless to say, this would not be an obstacle if it is held that Y did violate a rule as just mentioned.

### D. Case 4

As *supra*, Case 3.

---

53  *See* for details *Onrechtmatige Daad*, art. 163 (Van Maanen), aant. 15.
54  *See Onrechtmatige Daad* VI (Martens), No. 91.
55  *See Onrechtmatige Daad* VI (Martens), No. 81.
56  *See supra.*

## E. Case 5

D has probably committed a tort. His representation is a violation of a rule of unwritten law pertaining to proper social conduct. One should not make such representations if they are not true, the less if they aim to harm competitors.[57] Such a norm has the purpose also to protect P.

## F. Case 6

The answer is probably in the affirmative. In such a case we face a clash between the freedom of expression (Art. 10 ECHR) and protection of private life (Art. 8 ECHR).

The case comes fairly close to a case decided by the Supreme Court.[58] It was about G, who killed O during the war. After the war G was sent to prison, but he was granted a reprieve. After almost 50 years G was interviewed by a newspaper. He told the interviewer that his act was in the public interest (because the person who was killed was a great danger to the Dutch resistance). Hereafter, another newspaper published a couple of articles on the issue. In short it suggested that G. committed robbery with murder. G. sued the newspaper, which claimed, *inter alia*, that it had acted in the public interest.

The Court decided for G. The Supreme Court held that the facts took place long ago, that G had been in prison for some time; consequently, according to the Court, he had suffered the penalty.[59] Under these circumstances, taking the nature of the suspicion into account, one should be extremely reluctant to honour a defence as just mentioned, if it had to be honoured at all. The Court stressed that it was not inconceivable that the public interest could justify such statements, but only on persuasive grounds.

Applied to the present case, I tend to believe that the newspaper committed a tort (again, violation of a rule of unwritten law). The act happened 15 years ago, A suffered the punishment and became completely rehabilitated. In view of this, I do not think that the statements are in the public interest. Weighing the interests, A's have to prevail.

## G. Case 7

Since the issue has to be solved on the basis of tort law, the answer is along the lines of Case 5. The view is incorrect; P. knew – or should have known – so. The aim apparently is to harm D.

## H. Case 8

This case is borrowed from a fiercely criticized judgment of the Supreme Court.[60] The claim was *dismissed*. Pushing V is unlawful (a violation of a right and of a statutory

---

57  *See* for similar cases *Onrechtmatige Daad* VI (Martens), No. 162.
58  HR 6-1-1995, NJ 1995, 422 EJD.
59  A rather remarkable statement, bearing in mind that G was imprisoned for only a year and a half.
60  HR 31-3-1995, NJ 1997, 592 CJHB.

duty); however, V provoked the owner's action. Consequently, it was *not unlawful* in the present circumstances. It is not entirely clear how this judgment is to be interpreted. First, it could be argued that it says that the owner's conduct was not negligent. It could also be read as saying that there was a ground for justification, notably self-defence.

I have to admit that I doubt whether the argument is convincing. The owner put himself in this situation, knowing that V had drunk quite a lot of alcohol. He should have taken into account that V might have lost (a part of) his self-control. Or, let me give another example: D threatens P with a knife. P pulls his gun. D, afraid of being shot, stabs D. I do not believe that D could invoke self-defence.

Be that as it may, the Supreme Court held that the owner would not be liable anyway, even not if his conduct would be *unlawful*. In this case, V had to keep the damage entirely for his own account. In view of his contributory negligence, it would be unfair (not equitable) to require even a partial compensation from the owner! The outcome does not support the view, expressed above, that there is a clear trend to find ways to compensate victims, suffering personal injury. However, it should be stressed that this case is somewhat of an exception.[61]

## I. Case 9

This case should be viewed against the background of section VI. H. *supra*. B's and C's rights are violated. But, as mentioned *supra* in Section II, this is not necessarily enough to constitute a tort.

Assuming they faced a *permanent and severe* smell, while this situation did not exist at the time they moved to the spot, they have a fair chance of suing O for damages.[62] Producing such a smell violates a rule of unwritten law: it is in conflict with proper social conduct.[63] A's chances are less favourable than B's and C's; after all, it is very much open to debate whether A suffered damage in the sense of art. 6:95 BW.[64] A's chances would be better if the smell caused mental problems.[65]

As a general rule, a legally valid permit does *not* bar a claim. Whether it does in a specific case depends upon the character of the permit, the statute upon which it is based and the circumstances of the case.[66]

---

61   G.E. van Maanen assumes that the Supreme Court was influenced by truly calvinistic values: one
      should not eat and drink so exuberantly (NTBR 1996, p. 64).
62   The chance of getting a prohibition order against O is very remote in view of art. 6:168 BW.
63   *See* for case law *Onrechtmatige Daad* VIII.3 (Hartlief and Tjittes), aant. 19.
64   *See* for a more or less comparable example (a tour operator sells a 'once in a lifetime' holiday,
      which turns out to be of very poor quality): A.R. Bloembergen, *Nieuw BW monografie* B34, No.
      28.e. *See* for a different view J. van Schellen, RMThemis 1984, 412.
65   In that case, art. 6:106 sub b could bring relief; *see Schadevergoeding,* art. 106 (Deurvorst), aant. 30.
66   HR 10-3-1972, NJ 1972, 278 GJS. *See* for many details *Onrechtmatige Daad,* art. 162, lid 2
      (Jansen), aant. 79 ff.

## J. Case 10

(a) This topic is characterized by a (serious) danger which cannot be attributed to an action by D. Whether or not D is liable depends on the question as to whether he was aware of the seriousness of the danger.[67] It seems likely that the question has to be answered in the affirmative, in view of the seriousness of the risk involved.

(b) Our Criminal Code deals with this topic as well: art. 427. Yet, it follows from the above that one also has to face whether D's 'act' is in conflict with the requirements of proper social conduct. In the case of (serious) danger caused by one's acts, it comes down to the application of the following criteria: the likelihood of an accident and of the damage arising therefrom, the seriousness of the damage and the cost of taking precautionary measures.[68]

Applying these criteria, one may take it that D is liable, all the more so since case law shows a clear trend to protect victims suffering (serious) personal injury.

One could possibly argue that D did not act but 'only' failed to do so. Be it as it may, D cannot rely on this argument. He has to ensure that the hole remains properly fenced. If he becomes aware of the fact that it no longer is, he has to take action.

(c) Under Dutch law, one is required to help those who find themselves in acute danger to life (art. 450 Criminal Code). This is clearly the case. Consequently, D infringed a legal provision; moreover, his act is not commensurate with the requirements of proper social conduct.[69] The same would probably be true even if V's situation were not so terrible. It seems sufficient that he might suffer severe consequences in the case where he had no treatment.

## K. Case 11

This case is entirely about contract law, so I shall leave it aside.

Failure in the performance of a contractual obligation (non-compliance or improper compliance) can also be a tort, if the requirements of art. 6:162/163 are met, independently from the non-compliance or improper compliance.[70] On the basis of the facts, this is not the case.

The topic is of limited importance. The consequences in both cases are the same; section 6.1.10 about legal obligations to repair damage applies anyway.

## L. Case 12

(a) The same story as Case 11.

---

67   HR 22-11-1974, NJ 1975,149.
68   HR 5-11-1965, NJ 1966,136.
69   *Cf.* C.J.J.M. Stolker, *Van Arts naar Advocaat*, p. 61.
70   *See* for details C.A. Boukema, *Nieuw BW monografie* A21, No. 27 ff. In other cases, contract law prevails.

(b)  First, it is not very likely that the agreement will be void, certainly not for the reason mentioned. Still, I shall assume it is. In that case there is no agreement,[71] so the question arises as to whether D had to inform P. The answer is in the affirmative in the case where D was – or should have been – aware of the sore spot and the nasty consequences of brushing the dog. D had to reckon with the serious possibility that P, not knowing the spot, would be bitten by the dog and would be injured. Telling P would have been easy and would not have cost a penny. *See* section VI. A. *supra*.

## M. Case 13

As far as D is concerned, I do not think that she is liable.[72] D cannot be blamed; she was not aware nor could she have been aware of the incorrect labelling.[73] The same is true for the hospital.

The manufacturer can be sued on the basis of product liability. The relevant rules are based on strict liability (the EC directive) and have to be left aside.

---

71  I shall leave aside the doctrinal debate whether the agreement is non-existent: *see* for elaboration on this point J. Hijma, *Nietigheid en vernietigbaarheid van rechtshandelingen*, p. 51 ff. I shall also leave aside whether the void agreement could serve as a basis for a claim. Asser-Hartkamp II, No. 489 *in fine* (although not explicitly mentioning the issue) possibly answers the question in the affirmative. *See*, more generally, A.C. van Schaick, *Contractsvrijheid en nietigheid*, p. 248 ff.
72  Liability should be based on contract law, more specifically art. 7:466 ff. BW.
73  Art. 7:453 BW requires a lack of care, seen from the angle of a good and professional medical worker.

# South Africa

WRONGFULNESS IN SOUTH AFRICAN LAW OF DELICT

J. Neethling

## I. Requirement of Wrongfulness

*Recognition:* The South African law of delict definitely recognizes wrongfulness or unlawfulness – apart from the act (human conduct), causation (factual and legal), fault (intention or negligence) and damage (patrimonial as well as non-patrimonial) – as an essential requirement for a delict and therefore delictual liability.[1]

*Description:* In very general terms, wrongfulness may be described as the factual infringement of a legally recognised interest of a person in a legally reprehensible manner. This means that an act may be described as wrongful only when, firstly, it has as its consequence a harmful result, and, secondly, it took place in violation of a legal norm.[2]

*Determination:* The basic norm to be employed in this respect, is the *boni mores* (legal convictions of the community). The *boni mores* is an objective yardstick based on reasonableness. The question is whether, according to the legal convictions of the community and in the light of all the circumstances of the case, the defendant infringed the interests of the plaintiff in an unreasonable or reasonable manner. This entails an *ex post facto* weighing-up of the interest(s) which the defendant actually promoted with his

---

1   *See* in general Neethling, Potgieter and Visser, *Law of Delict* (1994), p. 4, pp. 29–111; *see* also Boberg, *The Law of Delict*, Vol. 1 Aquilian Liability (1984), p. 30 ff.; Van der Walt, *Delict: Principles and Cases* (1979), p. 20 ff.; Van der Merwe and Olivier, *Die Onregmatige Daad in die Suid-Afrikaanse Reg* (1989), p. 49 ff. In *Herschel* v. *Mrupe* 1954 3 SA 464 (A) 485 the Appellate Division regarded wrongfulness as 'an essential element' for delictual liability.

2   *See* Neethling, Potgieter and Visser, *Law of Delict* (1994), pp. 29–31. Although an act may in the abstract therefore be considered to be reprehensible, wrongfulness will not be present unless an interest (patrimonial or personality) has been infringed (*cf. Pinchen* v. *Santam Insurance Co. Ltd.* 1963 2 SA 254 (W)).

*H. Koziol (ed.), Unification of Tort Law: Wrongfulness*, 101–114.

act, and those which he actually infringed.[3] Various factors may play a role in the process of determining the reasonableness of the defendant's conduct:[4] these include the nature and extent of the harm and of the foreseeable or foreseen loss; the possible value to the defendant or to society of the harmful conduct; practical steps which could have been taken by the defendant to prevent the loss (here the probable success, the cost and the relative ease of the preventive measures are taken into account); the nature of the relationship between the parties; the fact that the defendant knew that his conduct would cause damage to the plaintiff; the motive of the defendant;[5] the legal position in other countries; ethical and moral issues; the values underlying the bill of fundamental rights in the Constitution 108 of 1996; as well as other considerations of public interest or public policy.[6]

The same weighing-up of conflicting interests is also encountered when considering the applicability of a ground justifying the infringement of a legal interest (such as private defence, necessity, provocation, consent, statutory authority, official capacity, power of chastisement; and with regard to defamation, truth and public interest, privilege and fair comment). In reality, recognized grounds of justification are thus nothing more than practical applications of the *boni mores* criterion to typical factual situations that appear regularly in practice.[7]

The practical application of the *boni mores* criterion is furthermore facilitated by two general principles, that is, that wrongfulness lies either in the infringement of a subjective right, or in the non-compliance with or breach of a legal duty to prevent damage. Five

---

3     *See* in general Neethling, Potgieter and Visser, *Law of Delict* (1994), pp. 31–38; Boberg, *The Law of Delict* (1984), p. 33 ff.; Van der Walt, *Delict: Principles and Cases* (1979), pp. 22–23; Neethling, Potgieter and Visser, *Neethling's Law of Personality* (1996), pp. 60–62; Van Heerden and Neethling, *Unlawful Competition* (1995), pp. 122-124. *See* also, e.g., *Minister van Polisie* v. *Ewels*, 1975 3 SA 590 (A) 597; *Administrateur, Natal* v. *Trust Bank van Afrika Bpk* 1979 3 SA 824 (A) 833-834; *Marais* v. *Richard* 1981 1 SA 1157 (A) 1168; *Schultz* v. *Butt* 1986 3 SA 667 (A) 679; *Financial Mail (Pty) Ltd.* v. *Sage Holdings Ltd.* 1993 2 SA 451 (A) 462; *Administrateur, Transvaal* v. *Van der Merwe* 1994 4 SA 347 (A) 358.

4     These factors will, of course, be taken into account in denying or establishing liability on the basis of the cases discussed *infra* (section IV).

5     Although the *boni mores is basically an objective test, subjective factors (such as motive and knowledge) may in exceptional cases be taken into consideration in determining wrongfulness (see* Neethling, Potgieter and Visser, *The Law of Delict* (1994), pp. 37–38; for examples, *see Bress Designs (Pty) Ltd.* v. *GY Lounge Suite Manufacturers (Pty) Ltd.* 1991 2 SA 455 (W) 475; *Aetiology Today CC t/a Somerset Schools* v. *Van Aswegen* 1992 1 SA 807 (W) 820; *Coronation Brick (Pty) Ltd.* v. *Strachan Construction Co. (Pty) Ltd.* 1982 4 SA 371 (D) 386).

6     *See* Neethling, Potgieter and Visser, *Law of Delict* (1994), pp. 36–42. For striking examples, *see Coronation Brick (Pty) Ltd.* v. *Strachan Construction Co. (Pty) Ltd.* 1982 4 SA 371 (D) 380-384; *Administrateur, Transvaal* v. *Van der Merwe* 1994 4 SA 347 (A) 361; *Hawker* v. *Life Offices Association of South Africa* 1987 3 SA 777 (C); *Deneys Reitz* v. *SA Commercial, Catering and Allied Workers Union* 1991 2 SA 685 (W). *See* further Van Aswegen 'Policy considerations in the law of delict', 1993 THRHR (Journal of Contemporary Roman-Dutch Law), 171 ff.; Corbett 'Aspects of the role of policy in the evolution of our common law', 1987 SALJ (South African Law Journal), 52 ff.

7     *See* Neethling, Potgieter and Visser, *Law of Delict* (1994), p. 66 ff.; *Neethling's Law of Personality* (1996), p. 62, p. 102 ff., p. 153 ff.; Van der Walt, *Delict: Principles and Cases* (1979), p. 40 ff.; Van der Merwe and Olivier, *Die Onregmatige Daad in die Suid-Afrikaanse Reg* (1989), p. 70 ff; Boberg, *The Law of Delict* (1984), p. 724 ff.; *Clarke* v. *Hurst* 1992 4 SA 630 (D) 650.

categories of subjective rights are distinguished, namely real rights, personality rights, personal rights, immaterial property rights and personal immaterial property rights.[8] A subjective right is infringed when the object of the right (legal interest) or the relationship between the holder of the right and the object is factually disturbed (usually by damaging or injuring the object) in a manner that is *contra bonos mores*. In certain instances the mere factual disturbance of a legal interest is regarded as *prima facie* wrongful, that is, the act is wrongful unless the defendant can prove a ground of justification for his conduct (for example, in the case of property rights and the right to physical integrity).[9]

Breach of a legal duty is first of all utilized to determine wrongfulness in instances of liability for omissions and pure economic loss (including liability for negligent misrepresentation and interference with a contractual relationship).[10] The impairment of the legal interest in these cases is not *prima facie* wrongful, probably because, according to the *boni mores* criterion, there is neither a general duty to prevent loss to others by positive conduct, nor a general duty to prevent pure economic loss. The imposition of such duties would probably place too heavy a burden on persons in society. Therefore one has to determine in each case whether there is a legal duty to act positively or a duty to avoid economic loss. Different factors may play a role in determining the legal duty in these two situations. The following factors are indicative of a legal duty to act positively (and therefore of a wrongful omission):[11] prior conduct creating a (potentially) dangerous situation (the *omissio per commissionem* rule); control of a dangerous object; statutory provisions; a special relationship between the parties; the particular office (profession) of the defendant; a contractual undertaking for the safety of a third party; and the creation of the impression that the interests of a third party will be protected. In cases of pure economic loss the following factors may play a role:[12] knowledge of the

---

8    See Neethling, Potgieter and Visser, *Law of Delict* (1994), pp. 39–40 and pp. 43–48; *Neethling's Law of Personality* (1996), p. 12 ff.; Van Heerden and Neethling, *Unlawful Competition* (1995), pp. 79–82; Van der Merwe and Olivier, *Die Onregmatige Daad in die Suid-Afrikaanse Reg* (1989), p. 54 ff.; *Universiteit van Pretoria* v. *Tommie Meyer Films (Edms)* Bpk 1977 4 SA 376 (T); *Clarke* v. *Hurst* 1992 4 SA 630 (D). See also the discussion *infra* under section II.

9    See *Neethling, Potgieter and Visser, Law of Delict* (1994), p. 39; *cf. Knop* v. *Johannesburg City Council* 1995 2 SA 1 (A) 26 (Neethling and Potgieter, 1995 THRHR, 530–531.

10   See Neethling, Potgieter and Visser, *Law of Delict* (1994), pp. 48–66 and pp. 280–296.

11   See Neethling, Potgieter and Visser, *Law of Delict* (1994), p. 48 ff.; Van der Walt, *Delict: Principles and Cases* (1979), p. 23 ff.; Boberg, *The Law of Delict* (1984), p. 30 ff.; Van der Merwe and Olivier, *Die Onregmatige Daad in die Suid-Afrikaanse Reg* (1989), p. 59 ff.; *see* also *Minister van Polisie* v. *Ewels* 1975 3 SA 590 (A); *Administrateur, Transvaal* v. *Van der Merwe* 1994 4 SA 347 (A); *Compass Motors Industries (Pty) Ltd.* v. *Callguard (Pty) Ltd.* 1990 2 SA 520 (W).

12   See Neethling, Potgieter and Visser, *Law of Delict* (1994), pp. 283–286; *see* also, e.g., *Coronation Brick (Pty) Ltd.* v. *Strachan Construction Co. (Pty) Ltd.* 1982 4 SA 371 (D); *Knop* v. *Johannesburg City Council* 1995 2 SA 1 (A); *Arthur E Abrahams and Gross* v. *Cohen* 1991 2 SA 301 (C); *Indac Electronics (Pty) Ltd.* v. *Volkskas Bank Ltd.* 1992 1 SA 783 (A); *Minister of Law and Order* v. *Kadir* 1995 1 SA 303 (A). Similar factors are also taken into account with regard to whether there was a legal duty to furnish correct information in the case of negligent misrepresentation (Neethling, Potgieter and Visser, *Law of Delict* (1994), pp. 288–290; *Administrateur, Natal* v. *Trust Bank van Afrika Bpk* 1979 3 SA 824 (A); *Siman and Co (Pty) Ltd.* v. *Barclays National Bank Ltd.* 1984 2 SA 888 (A); *International Shipping Co (Pty) Ltd.* v. *Bentley* 1990 1 SA 680 (A); *Standard*

defendant that his conduct would cause damage; statutory provisions; the availability of practical preventive steps; the calling or profession of the defendant; the extent of the loss suffered (whether the situation can lead to indeterminate liability); the inability of the plaintiff to protect himself; and the possibility that the defendant can obtain insurance cover.

Secondly, breach of a duty is utilized to determine wrongfulness in cases of breach of a statutory duty.[13] To establish wrongfulness, the plaintiff must prove that: the relevant statutory measure provided him with a private-law remedy; he is a person for whose benefit and protection the statutory duty was imposed; the nature of the harm and the manner in which it occurred are such as are contemplated by the enactment; the defendant in fact transgressed the statutory provision; and that there was a causal nexus between the transgression of the statutory provision and the harm.

In the final analysis the task of a judge in determining wrongfulness is to define and interpret the *boni mores* objectively in a particular instance, having regard to established legal rules and principles (as an expression of the *boni mores* in the past),[14] and the circumstances of the case, and weighing up the interests of the plaintiff and the defendant with reference to the relevant factors set out above.

*Wrongfulness and negligence:* Because of the application of the English law 'duty of care' doctrine by South African courts to determine negligence on occasion – an approach which is foreign to the principles of Roman-Dutch law – the test for wrongfulness is sometimes confused with the test for negligence[15] which, as indicated, is a separate, independent requirement for delictual liability.[16] This is especially the case where the 'duty of care' concept is employed as a synonym for the 'legal duty' concept

---

[Note 12 continued]
Chartered Bank of Canada v. Nedperm Bank Ltd. 1994 4 SA 747 (A)) and interference with a contractual relationship (Neethling, Potgieter and Visser, *Law of Delict* (1994), p. 296; *Lanco Engineering CC* v. *Aris Box Manufacturers (Pty) Ltd* 1993 4 SA 378 (D)).

13  *See* Neethling, Potgieter and Visser, *Law of Delict* (1994), pp. 64–66; *Da Silva* v. *Coutinho* 1971 3 SA 123 (A).

14  *See Schultz* v. *Butt* 1986 3 SA 667 (A) 679.

15  *See,* e.g., *Government of the Republic of South Africa* v. *Basdeo* 1996 1 SA 355 (A); Neethling, 1997 THRHR, 682 ff.; *see* also in general Neethling, Potgieter and Visser, *Law of Delict* (1994), pp. 139–140.

16  *See* in regard to negligence Neethling, Potgieter and Visser, *Law of Delict* (1994), pp. 121 ff. The most authoritative statement on the test for negligence in South African law appears from the following *dictum* in *Kruger v Coetzee* 1966 2 SA 428 (A) 430:
'For the purposes of liability *culpa* arises if –
(a) a *diligens pater familias* in the position of the defendant –
    (i)  would foresee the reasonable possibility of his conduct injuring another in his person or property and causing him patrimonial loss; and
    (ii) would take reasonable steps to guard against such occurrence; and
(b) and the defendant failed to take such steps.
This has been constantly stated by this Court for some 50 years. Requirement (a)(ii) is sometimes overlooked. Whether a *diligens pater familias* in the position of the person concerned would take any guarding steps at all and, if so, what steps would be reasonable, must always depend on the particular circumstances of each case. No hard and fast rules can be laid down.'

as used in determining wrongfulness. To avoid confusion, the following factors are of importance to distinguish between wrongfulness and negligence:[17]

(i) wrongfulness is determined with reference to the *boni mores* – negligence with reference to the *bonus pater familias* or reasonable man (reasonable foreseeability and preventability of damage);

(ii) wrongfulness qualifies the act – negligence the actor;

(iii) wrongfulness is determined on the basis of actual facts or realities – negligence on the basis of probabilities.

## II. Nature of Interests Protected by Law of Delict

The nature of the interests protected by the South African law of delict is to a large extent determined by the doctrine of subjective rights. As stated, a fundamental premise is that wrongfulness consists of the infringement of a subjective right.[18]

The nature of a subjective right is largely determined by the nature of the object of the particular right (i.e., the interest concerned).[19] Thus rights are categorised and named with reference to the different types of legal objects to which the rights relate. Five classes or categories of rights are distinguished on this basis, namely real rights, personality rights, personal rights, immaterial property rights and personal immaterial property rights. The objects of these rights are respectively *property or things* (tangible objects such as a farm, a car, a pen, a flock of sheep and compressed air in a cylinder); *aspects of personality* (aspects of human personality such as physical integrity, physical freedom, good name or reputation, dignity or honour, privacy, identity and feelings);[20] *acts or performances* (human acts or conduct which may juridically be claimed from another, such as delivery by the seller of the thing sold, payment of the amount owing by the debtor, rendering of services by an employee, payment of maintenance); *immaterial property* (intangible products of the human mind, intellect and activity which are expressed in one or other outwardly perceptible form, such as patents, objects of copyright, designs, goodwill, trade secrets, distinctive marks and advertising marks);[21]

---

17  *See* also *Administrateur, Natal* v. *Trust Bank van Afrika* 1979 3 SA 824 (A) 833; *Knop* v. *Johannesburg City Council* 1995 2 SA 1 (A) 27; *S* v. *Robson; S* v. *Hattingh* 1991 3 SA 322 (W) 333; *Simon's Town Municipality* v. *Dews* 1993 1 SA 191 (A) 196 where Corbett CJ referred with approval to the 'modern distinctions in our law of delict between fault and unlawfulness'. *See* also Neethling, Potgieter and Visser, *Law of Delict* (1994), pp. 143–145; *cf.* Van der Merwe and Olivier, *Die Onregmatige Daad in die Suid-Afrikaanse Reg* (1989), p. 131; Boberg, *The Law of Delict* (1984), pp. 38–40.

18  *See supra* section I.

19  *See* Neethling, Potgieter and Visser, *Law of Delict* (1994), pp. 44–45; Van der Merwe and Olivier, *Die Onregmatige Daad in die Suid Afrikaanse Reg* (1989), p. 54 ff.; Van der Walt, *Delict: Principles and Cases* (1979), p. 22; *Universiteit van Pretoria* v. *Tommie Meyer Films (Edms) Bpk* 1977 4 SA 376 (T) 382.

20  *See* also *Neethling's Law of Personality* (1996), p. 27 ff.

21  *See* also Van Heerden and Neethling, *Unlawful Competition* (1995), p. 93 ff., p. 106 ff., pp. 216–219, p. 223 ff.

and *personal immaterial property* (intangible products of the human mind or endeavour which are connected with the personality, such as earning capacity and credit-worthiness).[22]

Apart from these identified and delimited interests, protection is also afforded against so-called pure economic loss in certain circumstances.[23] By the concept 'pure economic loss' is meant, on the one hand, patrimonial loss that does not result from damage to property or impairment of personality. On the other hand, pure economic loss refers to financial loss that does in fact flow from damage to property or impairment of personality, but which does not involve the plaintiff's property or person; or if it does, the defendant did not cause such damage or injury.

Pure economic loss and financial loss as a result of the infringement of an identified interest may, of course, overlap. For example, owning to the pure financial nature of the interests concerned in cases of interference with a contractual relationship (where performance is at stake), prejudice almost always takes the form of pure economic loss.[24] Similarly, this will be the case in most instances of unlawful competition where goodwill is involved.[25]

The importance for the law of delict of identifying protected interests is that it increases our ability to articulate and apply principles of legal protection because we become certain what it is that compels us towards protective measures and wherein the interest concerned differs from what has already been recognised or refused recognition under established legal theory.[26]

## III. Borderline between Delict and Contract

Breach of contract clearly constitutes a form of wrongful conduct in private law. As with a delict, breach of contract is an act by one person (contracting party) which in a wrongful and culpable way causes damage to another (contracting party). Thus there is no material difference between these two legal phenomena.[27]

Nevertheless, breach of contract and a delict are fundamentally different.[28] Breach of contract is constituted only by the non-fulfilment by a contractual party of a contractual personal right (claim) or an obligation to perform. Accordingly, the primary

---

22  *See also Neethling's Law of Personality* (1996), pp. 19–23; Neethling 'Persoonlike immaterieel-goedereregte: 'n Nuwe kategorie subjektiewe regte?' 1987 THRHR, 316 ff.

23  *See* Neethling, Potgieter and Visser, *Law of Delict* (1994), p. 280 ff.; Boberg, *The Law of Delict* (1984), p. 103 ff.; Van der Walt, *Delict: Principles and Cases* (1979), pp. 35–37; *supra* fn 12.

24  *See* Neethling, Potgieter and Visser, *Law of Delict* (1994), p. 296.

25  Van Heerden and Neethling, *Unlawful Competition* (1995), *passim*.

26  *Cf.* Gross, 'The concept of privacy' 1967 NYULR (*New York University Law Review*), 34, with regard to privacy; *Neethling's Law of Personality* (1996), p. 28.

27  *See* Neethling, Potgieter and Visser, *Law of Delict* (1994), p. 6; Burchell, *Principles of Delict* (1993), p. 3 ff.; *Lillicrap, Wassenaar and Partners* v. *Pilkington Brothers (SA) (Pty) Ltd.* 1985 1 SA 475 (A) 495–496.

28  *See* Van Aswegen *Die Sameloop van Eise om Skadevergoeding uit Kontrakbreuk en Delik* (1991) (LLD-thesis University of South Africa), p. 300 ff.

remedy for breach of contract is directed at enforcement, fulfilment or execution of the contract; a claim for damages as a remedy only plays a secondary role. On the other hand, a delict is constituted by the infringement of any legally recognised interest of another, excluding the non-fulfilment of a duty to perform by a contractual party. Consequently, the delictual remedies are primarily directed at damages (or satisfaction) and not at fulfilment. The fundamental differences between breach of contract and a delict are for historical, systematic and practical reasons also supported by the fact that breach of contract is not formally treated as part of the law of delict but is considered as part of the law of contract. The law of contract, as has been indicated, then provides specific rules and remedies in regard to breach of contract which are not applicable to a delict. This distinction is clearly apparent from the fact that one and the same act may render the wrongdoer liable *ex contractu* as well as *ex delicto*.

This will, however, only be the case if, apart from breach of contract, the conduct complained of also wrongfully and culpably infringes a legally protected interest which exists independently of the contract. Take the following example: a surgeon agrees with the patient to operate on him. He does not perform the operation properly and the patient's health is affected. In the first place, the surgeon commits a breach of contract because he has not performed in accordance with the agreement. However, he also commits a delict because, irrespective of the contract, he has infringed the patient's right to physical integrity.[29] According to Van Aswegen[30] the test that should be employed *de lege ferenda* to determine whether independent delictual liability is present, is to eliminate mentally the validity of the contract, but not the particular factual relationship between the parties.

In this connection it appears that the courts – unlike the position where a breach of contract also causes, for example, damage to property or an injury to personality – will not readily construe an interest that exists independently of the contract in cases of pure economic loss. In the case of the negligent provision of professional services in terms of an agreement (by, for example, attorneys, auditors and architects) the wronged person will thus as a rule only have the contractual action at his disposal.[31]

Where there is a concurrence of a delictual and a contractual claim with regard to patrimonial loss, the aggrieved party may elect either to base his claim on delict, or breach of contract, or both. Different factors may play a role in determining his choice of whether to claim *ex contractu* or *ex delicto* (Aquilian action). On this basis he can then choose the action which will be the most advantageous to him. These factors are the following:[32]

---

29  See *Lillicrap, Wassenaar and Partners* v. *Pilkington Brothers (SA) (Pty) Ltd*. 1985 1 SA 475 (A) 496 499; *Van Wyk* v. *Lewis* 1924 AD 438; Van der Walt, *Delict: Principles and Cases* (1979), p. 7.

30  Van Aswegen, *Die Sameloop van Eise om Skadevergoeding uit Kontrakbreuk en Delik* (1991), p. 298; *cf.* Midgley 'Concurrent claims: Tests for establishing independent liability in delict', 1993 SALJ, 66 ff.

31  *Cf. Lillicrap, Wassenaar and Partners* v. *Pilkington Brothers (SA) (Pty) Ltd*. 1985 1 SA 475 (A) 499–500; Neethling, Potgieter and Visser, *Law of Delict* (1994), p. 253 fn 65.

32  See *Die Sameloop van Eise om Skadevergoeding uit Kontrakbreuk en Delik* (1991), p. 452 ff.; Neethling, Potgieter and Visser, *Law of Delict* (1994), pp. 254–255.

(i)   The extent of damages recoverable can differ because different measures limiting liability apply;

(ii)  the time for the computation of damages in the two instances differs;

(iii) the requirements for the capacity of legal subjects for the two types of liability are such that, in a given case, a legal subject can 'qualify' for delictual liability but not for liability for breach of contract;

(iv)  the liability of joint delictual wrongdoers differs from that of joint parties to a contract;

(v)   vicarious liability differs in the two instances in so far as it can be more extensive in the case of delict than for breach of contract;

(vi)  unilateral waiver of his rights by a prejudiced party can extinguish the (possible) liability of a delictual wrongdoer, as is the case with consent, whereas unilateral waiver of a contractual right to performance cannot extinguish the other contracting party's obligation to perform;

(vii) a contractual term excluding or limiting liability may, depending on the interpretation thereof, apply only to contractual liability – a penalty clause will also probably not apply to delictual liability;

(viii)contributory negligence can only be raised against a delictual claim;

(ix)  the onus of proof may differ in respect of contractual and delictual claims;

(x)   different courts can have jurisdiction in claims for delict and breach of contract respectively; and

(xi)  the rules of private international law or conflict of laws differ in respect of these two types of claims.

Finally, reference must be made to the situation where damages result from a negligent misrepresentation inducing a contract. According to the Appellate Division[33] there is in principle no distinction between a misrepresentation which induces a contract and one made outside the contractual sphere. A negligent misrepresentation may therefore, depending on the circumstances and provided that all the requirements for delictual liability are present, give rise to a delictual claim for damages even though the misrepresentation induced the plaintiff to conclude a contract with the party who made it.

## IV. The Cases

### A. Case 1

D's conduct constitutes unlawful competition. Interference with a rival's business, not for the purpose of promoting D's business interests, but for reasons of personal vindictiveness and with the sole or dominant purpose to drive P out of business, is considered to be an unreasonable infringement of P's (subjective) right to the goodwill of his business and thus

---

33   *Bayer South Africa (Pty) Ltd.* v. *Frost* 1991 4 SA 559 (A).

to be wrongful.[34] Malice or improper motive is therefore a strong indication of the unreasonableness (wrongfulness) of damage-causing conduct in South African law and is regarded as an application of the doctrine of abuse of rights (*abus de droit*).[35]

## B. Case 2

The interference by a third party (D) with a contractual relationship causing one of the contracting parties (X) to commit breach of contract, constitutes a wrongful act by D against the other contracting party (P). However, according to South African case law only an intentional interference is actionable; it is still uncertain whether a negligent interference will also constitute a delict.[36] (This principle also applies in the field of unlawful competition, as is the case with regard to D and P.)[37] Be that as it may, since this case is also concerned with liability for pure economic loss, the wrongfulness of the interference with the contractual relationship (between X and P) should be judged in the light of the *boni mores* criterion, taking into account factors such as the knowledge of the defendant of the existence of the contract.[38]

## C. Case 3

It is generally accepted in the South African law of delict that breach of a statutory duty resulting in damage to a person, is wrongful provided that certain requirements are met, *inter alia,* that the nature of the harm and the manner in which it occurred are such as is contemplated by the statute.[39] It stands to reason that this requirement is not complied with as the purpose of the traffic statute was not to protect X against the economic loss caused by Y's breach thereof. Breach of the statutory provision *in casu* may, however, amount to unlawful competition, because Y's conduct transgresses the equality principle of the law of competition, namely the *par conditio concurrentium*.[40]

---

34  See *Bress Designs (Pty) Ltd.* v. *GY Lounge Suite Manufacturers (Pty) Ltd.* 1991 2 SA 455 (W) 475-476; *see* also Neethling, Potgieter and Visser, *Law of Delict* (1994), p. 300; Van Heerden and Neethling, *Unlawful Competition* (1995), pp. 139-140.

35  See Neethling, Potgieter and Visser, *Law of Delict* (1994), pp. 104–110, p. 106 fn 449; Van Heerden and Neethling, *Unlawful Competition* (1995), pp. 135–140.

36  See *Union Government* v. *Ocean Accident and Guarantee Corporation Ltd.* 1956 1 SA 577 (A); *cf. Dantex Investment Holdings (Pty) Ltd.* v. *Brenner* 1989 1 SA 390 (A) 395; *Lanco Engineering CC* v. *Aris Box Manufacturing (Pty) Ltd.* 1993 4 SA 378 (D); *see* further Neethling, Potgieter and Visser, *Law of Delict* (1994), pp. 293–296.

37  See e.g. *Atlas Organic Fertilizers (Pty) Ltd.* v. *Pikkewyn Ghwano (Pty) Ltd.* 1981 2 SA 173 (T) 202; *see* also Van Heerden and Neethling, *Unlawful Competition* (1995), pp. 257-260.

38  See Neethling, Potgieter and Visser, *Law of Delict* (1994), p. 296; *cf. Lanco Engineering CC* v. *Aris Box Manufacturing (Pty) Ltd.* 1993 4 SA 378 (D) 380 384 where the *boni mores* test was actually applied; *cf.* also *supra* section I.

39  See *Da Silva* v. *Coutinho* 1971 3 SA 123 (A) 140; Neethling, Potgieter and Visser, *Law of Delict* (1994), pp. 64–66; *supra* section I.).

40  See Neethling, Potgieter and Visser, *Law of Delict* (1994), p. 303; Van Heerden and Neethling, *Unlawful Competition* (1995), pp. 266–281.

## D. Case 4

It seems that this case is similar to Case 3, that is, the breach of the statutory duty was not *per se* wrongful since neither was the plaintiff (P) a person for whose benefit the legislation was imposed, nor was the nature of the harm and the manner in which it occurred, contemplated by the statute.[41] If D was a competitor of P, his supplying of oil in transgression of the legislation would nevertheless amount to unlawful competition against P (see Case 3). However, if D was not acting in competition with P, the wrongfulness D's act causing pure economic loss to P will have to be ascertained by applying the *boni mores* test and taking into account the factors that can play al role in this regard, *inter alia* whether D knew that P was supplying oil to Ruritania and would suffer damage as a result of his covert supplying of oil to the rebels.[42]

## E. Case 5

Deception or misrepresentation of the public or a third party as to a competitor's own performance – D's dishonest misrepresentations as to his business background – is a form of unlawful competition in South African law.[43] The ordinary delictual action based on (intentional) misrepresentation is, however, not available since it is required that P – and not a third party – must have been misled as a result of the misrepresentation.[44]

## F. Case 6

Allegations placing a person's moral character in a bad light, such as that he has been guilty of criminal behaviour or was dishonest, are considered to be *prima facie* defamatory in South African law, and therefore in principle wrongful (infringement of the right to good name or reputation). However, such wrongfulness may be rebutted by proving that the allegations were true and in the public interest. It has already been decided by South African courts that transgressions which occurred a long time ago should not be raked up, that is, that public interest would suffer rather than benefit by the unnecessary revival of forgotten scandals.[45] It therefore seems that despite the fact that the allegations were entirely correct, the publication by B of the defamatory remarks about A was not in the public interest and consequently wrongful.

---

41  *See* again *supra* section I.
42  *See supra* section I.
43  *See*, e.g., *Long John International Ltd.* v. *Stellenbosch Wine Trust (Pty) Ltd.* 1990 4 SA 136 (D); *Spinner Communications* v. *Argus Newspapers Ltd.* 1996 4 SA 637 (W); Van Heerden and Neethling, *Unlawful Competition* (1995), pp. 149–163; Neethling, Potgieter and Visser, *Law of Delict* (1994), p. 301.
44  Neethling, Potgieter and Visser, *Law of Delict* (1994), p. 292.
45  *See* e.g. *Graham* v. *Ker* (1892) 9 SC 185 187; *Kemp* v. *Republican Press (Pty) Ltd.* 1994 4 SA 261 (E); *see* further *Neethling's Law of Personality* (1996), p. 151, and p. 167; Neethling, Potgieter and Visser, *Law of Delict* (1994), p. 326.

## G. Case 7

In South African law a statement casting suspicion on a person's vocational capacities or competence – such as D's statement that P was an unreliable employee – is *prima facie* defamatory (wrongful).[46] Such wrongfulness may be rebutted by proving that D made it on a privileged occasion, that is, that he had a legal, moral or social duty, or legitimate interest, to make the defamatory remark to X who had a corresponding duty or interest to learn of the remark. It has been decided that passing on information on the character of a potential employee by a former to a future employer was privileged, even if it was inaccurate, provided that it was relevant to the discharge of the duty or interest concerned, and that it was not made with malice.[47]

## H. Case 8

Infringement of a person's right to physical integrity by causing him personal injuries (such as in the case of V) is *prima facie* wrongful,[48] but the owner may prove the existence of a ground of justification rebutting such wrongfulness. However, it does not seem that the owner will be able to justify his conduct since the only possible ground, namely private defence,[49] is excluded because of the fact that the owner did not defend himself against an unlawful attack on the part of V. (V was leaving the restaurant lawfully, having paid the bill in full. He was in fact defending himself – by making the gesture with his arm – against an unlawful restriction of his freedom by the owner.) The owner's push of V and his subsequent injuries were therefore wrongful. Because of his impression that the doctors were leaving the restaurant without paying, the owner may further aver that he acted in putative private defence. This is a ground excluding fault (intent – because the owner was not conscious of the wrongfulness of his conduct; or negligence – because the owner acted as a reasonable man would have done in the circumstances).

## I. Case 9

For the purposes of this case it is assumed that the production of the oil products is forbidden by statute unless the actor has a valid permit.

(a) If O has a valid permit, and therefore statutory authority to produce the oil products, his infringement of A (sensory feelings) and B's (health) physical integrity,[50] or C's economic loss is not wrongful provided that he exercised his authority in a reasonable

---

46  *Neethling's Law of Personality* (1996), pp. 152–153.
47  *Couldridge* v. *Eskom* 1994 1 SA 91 (SE); *see* also Neethling, Potgieter and Visser, *Law of Delict* (1994), pp. 324–325; *Neethling's Law of Personality* (1996), pp. 157–161.
48  *See* e.g. *Minister of Justice* v. *Hofmeyr* 1993 3 SA 131 (A) 145-146 153; *Neethling's Law of Personality* (1996), pp. 101–102.
49  *See* Neethling, Potgieter and Visser, *Law of Delict* (1994), pp. 68–77; *Neethling's Law of Personality* (1996), pp. 102–104.
50  *Neethling's Law of Personality* (1996), pp. 90–94.

(lawful) manner. This will be the case if it was impossible for him to produce the products without infringing the interests concerned, and it was furthermore impossible to prevent or minimise the damage by taking reasonable precautions.[51] If O exceeded his statutory authority in any of these respects, the causing of damage by his smell-producing activities is wrongful (see also (b) below).

(b) If O does not have a valid permit, his damage-causing conduct is in breach of a statutory duty.[52] The infringement of the physical integrity of A and B is then wrongful. As far as C is concerned, the fact that pure economic loss was caused in breach of a statutory duty, may be an indication of the existence of a legal duty not to cause such loss, and therefore of wrongfulness.[53]

If the activities of O are not prohibited by statute, the causing of harm to A, B and C may still be considered to be wrongful nuisance,[54] that is, the unreasonable use of land by the owner at the expense of another (A, B and C). To determine the reasonableness or not of O's conduct, the ordinary test for wrongfulness must be applied, namely the benefit gained by O must be weighed up against the loss suffered by the others.

## J.  Case 10

All three cases are concerned with liability for an omission. As a general rule in South African law, a person does not act wrongfully where he fails to act positively to prevent harm to another. Wrongfulness will only be present if in the particular circumstances there was a legal duty on the defendant to prevent such harm, and he failed to comply with that duty. The question whether such a duty exits, is answered with reference to the *boni mores* criterion. Several factors which have already crystallised in the courts, point to the existence of a duty to act positively and may thus facilitate the application of the *boni mores* test.[55]

(a) In accordance with the *boni mores* test, a balancing process must take place between the interests of D (inconvenience and trouble to warn) and that of the blind person (serious personal injuries). It must then be decided whether D's omission to warn does not merely evoke moral indignation, but should also be regarded as wrongful according to the legal convictions of the community. Here it will probably be decided that there was a legal duty on D to warn the blind person, because he knew of the dangerous situation and could have warned him with ease.[56]

---

51  Neethling, Potgieter and Visser, *Law of Delict* (1994), pp. 97–99; *cf. Simon's Town Municipality* v. *Dews* 1993 1 SA 191 (A).
52  *See supra* section I as to the question of wrongfulness in this regard.
53  See *Knop* v. *Johannesburg City Council* 1995 2 SA 1 (A) 31 33; *see* also *supra* section I as regards wrongfulness in cases of pure economic loss.
54  *See* Neethling, Potgieter and Visser, *Law of Delict* (1994), pp. 110–111; Van der Merwe and Olivier, *Die Onregmatige Daad in die Suid-Afrikaanse Reg* (1989), p. 506.
55  *See Minister van Polisie* v. *Ewels* 1975 3 SA 590 (A) 597; Neethling, Potgieter and Visser, *Law of Delict* (1994), p. 50 ff.; *supra* section I.
56  *Cf.* Neethling, Potgieter and Visser, *Law of Delict* (1994), pp. 63–64.

(b) Two of the factors which play a role to determine the existence of a legal duty, are the creation by the defendant through prior conduct of a potentially dangerous situation (*omissio per commissionem*), and knowledge by the defendant of the existence of such a situation. In this case the combination of these two factors will probably create a legal duty on the part of D to safeguard the hole, the failure of which resulting in P's injuries will constitute a wrongful omission.

(c) There is no general duty on a doctor in South African law to treat persons in need of medical attention. The following factors may, however, indicate the existence of a legal duty to treat P – and therefore wrongfulness – on the part of D:

(1) D's actual knowledge of P's condition;
(2) the seriousness of P's condition;
(3) the professional ability of D to do what is asked of him;
(4) the physical state of D himself;
(5) the availability of other doctors, or even of nurses and paramedics;
(6) the interests of other patients;
(7) whether attending P would expose D to danger;
(8) whether D is desirous to be treated or not; and
(9) professional ethical considerations.[57]

*In casu* the scale seems to favour a finding that there was a legal duty on D.

## K. Case 11

D will in principle be delictually liable for the economic loss he caused to P if P can prove that he was induced by a (negligent) misrepresentation – albeit in the form of an omission (non-disclosure of material information)[58] – on D's part to conclude the agreement.[59] The crucial question as to wrongfulness is whether there was a legal duty on D to furnish the correct information to P. Whether such a duty exists, is again dependent on the *boni mores*, where the following factors – which have crystallised in the courts – point to the existence of such a duty on D's part: the contractual relationship between D and P; D had specific information in his exclusive possession by reason of his particular occupation, and this information could therefore not be obtained in another manner than from D (or an associate); D, who by reason of his particular occupation claimed to command professional knowledge and competence, furnished the information in a professional capacity; D knew at the time he furnished the information that P

---

57 *See* Neethling 'Professionele aanspreeklikheid teenoor derdes', 1996 THRHR, pp. 194–195; Strauss, *Doctor, Patient and the Law* (1991), p. 25.
58 *McCann* v. *Goodall Group Operations (Pty) Ltd.* 1995 2 SA 718 (C).
59 *See Bayer South Africa (Pty) Ltd.* v. *Frost* 1991 4 SA 559 (A); Neethling, Potgieter and Visser, *Law of Delict* (1994), pp. 286–293; *see* also *supra* section III.

would rely on it; and liability would not lead to a multiplicity of actions that could be socially calamitous.[60]

## L. Case 12

(a)  Where the contract is valid, apart from a possible claim based on breach of contract, there may also be a concurrent delictual claim if, apart from breach of contract, the conduct complained of also wrongfully and culpably infringes a legally protected interest of P which exists independently of the contract. P may then elect either to base his claim on delict, or breach of contract, or both.[61] As far as the delictual claim is concerned, the question is whether there was a legal duty on D to tell P of the dog's sore spot (liability for an omission: see Case 10 above), the breach of which led to a wrongful infringement of P's physical integrity – an interest which exists independently of the contract between D and P. Two factors seem to indicate such a duty: first of all, the contractual relationship between the parties; and secondly, the fact that D knew of the sore spot and therefore of the existence of a dangerous situation that could lead to the dog biting P.[62]

(b)  If the contract is invalid, P has the delictual claim only at his disposal, also based on liability for an omission (as explained under (a) above). (However, here the special relationship between the parties is not based on a valid contract.)[63]

## M. Case 13

D infringed P's right to physical integrity (causing ill health) without justification by injecting him with the wrong concentration of the medicine. D's act is therefore wrongful. D will, however, not be delictually liable because of absence of fault, provided that she did not know that the information on the label was incorrect (absence of intention or *dolus*), and that a reasonable man in her position would also not have known this (absence of negligence). The manufacturer of the medicine, assuming that it also labelled the medicine, may be delictually liable on the basis of a defective product causing harm.[64]

---

60    *See* Neethling, Potgieter and Visser, *Law of Delict* (1994), pp. 288–289; *see* also the following cases: *McCann* v. *Goodall Group Operations (Pty) Ltd.* 1995 4 SA 718 (C); *Standard Chartered Bank of Canada* v. *Nedperm Bank Ltd.* 1994 4 SA 747 (A); *Siman and Co. (Pty) Ltd.* v. *Barclays National Bank Ltd.* 1984 2 SA 888 (A); *Lillicrap, Wassenaar and Partners* v. *Pilkington Brothers (SA) (Pty) Ltd.* 1985 1 SA 475 (A); *International Shipping Co. (Pty) Ltd.* v. *Bentley* 1990 1 SA 680 (A); *Bayer South Africa (Pty) Ltd.* v. *Frost* 1991 4 SA 559 (A).

61    *See supra* section III.

62    *See* Neethling, Potgieter and Visser, *Law of Delict* (1994), p. 57 fn 126, pp. 60–61.

63    *In casu* P may, apart from basing his delictual claim on the *actio legis Aquiliae* for which negligence is a requirement, also base his claim on the *actio de pauperie*, an action creating strict liability for the owner of a domestic animal which caused damage (*see* Neethling, Potgieter and Visser, *Law of Delict* (1994), pp. 343–346).

64    *See* Neethling, Potgieter and Visser, *Law of Delict* (1994), pp. 304–308.

# Switzerland

FUNCTION AND RELEVANCE UNDER SWISS LAW

Pierre Widmer

## I. Statutory Bases

### A. Civil Code (Code of Obligations)

'Wrongfulness' or 'unlawfulness' ('*Widerrechtlichkeit*' or '*Rechtswidrigkeit*' in German,[1] '*illicéité*' in French '*illecito/illiceità*' in Italian) is mentioned as a condition of liability in Article 41 of the Swiss Code of Obligations (SCO; SR/RS [Systematic Digest of Swiss Federal Legislation] 220) which states the general clause of liability for fault:

A. Liability in General    Art.41 1 Whoever causes damage to another person *in*
I. Requirements of liability *an unlawful way*, be it wilfully or be it by negligence, is
liable for compensation.
2 Whoever, contra bonos mores, wilfully causes damage
to another person is also liable for compensation.

'Unlawfulness' is in this context considered as the second of three general and indispensable prerequisites for liability: the first logically being damage, and the third causation. According to a majority view in doctrine, these three general conditions are also operational in the field of strict liability.[2] One can therefore say, that unlawfulness – like the existence of a damage and of a causal link between the damage and the relevant

---

1    In Swiss juridical literature, '*Widerrechtlichkeit*' and '*Rechtswidrigkeit*' are used as synonymous expressions; the Code of Obligations (SCO Art.41, 49) prefers the adverb '*widerrechtlich*', but there are other provisions where the term '*rechtswidrig*' also appears (e.g., SCO Art. 100 para. 1).
2    As far as 'unlawfulness' is concerned *see*: Oftinger/Stark, *Schweiz. Haftpflichtrecht*, Bd.I. Allgemeiner Teil (5.Aufl. 1995), Zürich, § 4, p. 165 ff. (No. 55/56, p. 186 f.); *idem, Schweiz. Haftpflichtrecht*, Bd.II/2: Gefährdungshaftungen (4th ed. 1989), Zürich, § 24, No. 27 ff., p. 11 ff.; A. Keller, *Haftpflicht im Privatrecht*, (5th ed. 1993), Berne, p. 89; Rey, *Ausservertragliches Haftpflichtrecht* (1995), Zürich, § 6, No. 669; opposite opinion: Deschenaux/Tercier, *La responsabilité civile* (2nd ed. 1982), Berne, § 2, No. 24, p. 41; Gauch, 'Grundbegriffe des ausservertraglichen Haftungsrechts', in: *recht* 6/96, 225 ff. (233 ff.). Question left open in DFC [Decisions of the Federal Court] 116 [1990] II 480 ff. ("Chernobyl-Case").

*H. Koziol (ed.), Unification of Tort Law: Wrongfulness, 115–127.*

fact (the so-called '*Anknüpfungstatbestand*', which can be a human behaviour or an objectively determined situation) is a Janus-faced element which may, in a positive sense, create liability as well as it is able – in a negative way – to exclude or to limit it.

It may be of a certain interest to note that the term 'unlawful' in the text of the above-mentioned provision is used as a qualifying (or, rather, disqualifying) adverb for 'the way in which a person causes damage to another'. This syntactical argument could be used to defend a theory according to which 'unlawfulness' has to be conceived as an element of human conduct ('*Verhaltensunrecht*') rather than as a characteristic of the attempt to someone's interests, resp. the result of such attempt ('*Erfolgsunrecht*'). The grammatical aspect is not without significance when comparing the Swiss with the Italian code. In fact, art. 2043 of the Italian Civil Code speaks of '*danno illecito*' = '*unlawful damage*' and – as Busnelli and Comandé show in their paper[3] – the recent Italian doctrine has taken advantage of that particular structure of the sentence in order to develop a 'functional *concept of* indemnity as compensation rather than sanction'.

The two mentioned codes have, however, also a common characteristic in that they both (as well as the Austrian ABGB in its § 1295) try to combine the French general clause with the German approach (§ 823 para. 1 BGB) based on an enumeration of the interests which deserve legal protection ('*Rechtsgüter*'). The influence of the German model is also clearly identifiable in para.2 of Art. 41 COS (as well as in § 1295 para. 2 ABGB) which reproduces almost literally the text of § 826 BGB; this kind of escape clause or safety-valve based on a violation of standards of morality (*bonos mores*) is typical of systems with a relatively restrictive definition of tort.[4]

## B. Special Legislation

'Unlawfulness' also plays an implicit role in several special acts[5] which establish particular rules of liability for determinate risks. Some of these acts expressly state that their special liability provisions (regularly setting up strict liability) apply only to personal injury and damage to objects; this is considered to be a 'qualified silence' of the legislator from which it follows that other types of damage, in particular 'pure economic loss', is not covered.[6] An example of such a provision is Art. 58 para. 1 of the Road Traffic Act[7] which reads as follows:

---

3   'Wrongfulness' in the Italian Legal System, p. 4. after fn.6.
4   *See* Oftinger/Stark, *Schweiz. Haftpflichtrecht*, Bd.II/1 Verschuldenshaftung, gewöhnliche Kausal-haftungen (4.Aufl. 1987), Zürich, § 16/4, p. 16 ff., No. 41 ff. (No. 191 ff., p.61 ff.).
5   *See* Widmer, 'Détermination et réduction de la réparation en droit suisse', in Spier (ed.), *The Limits of Liability* (1996), The Hague, p. 137 ff. (p.139 f., fn. 11 and 17).
6   *See* in particular Werro, 'Tort liability for pure economic loss - A critique of current trends in Swiss law', in Banakas (ed.), *Civil Liability for Pure Economic Loss*, (1996), The Hague, p. 181 ff.; *idem*, 'Die Sorgfaltspflichtverletzung als Haftungsgrund nach Art. 41 OR', ZSR [*Zeitschrift für Schweizerisches Recht*] 116 [1997] I p. 343 ff.
7   Strassenverkehrsgesetz/Loi sur la circulation routière (SR/RS 741.01). *See* also DFC 106 [1980] II 75 ff.

Art. 58    1. Where a *person is killed or injured* or where *property is damaged* by a motor
vehicle in operation, the holder of the vehicle is liable for compensation.

Similar provisions can be found in the Railway Liability Act, the Electricity Act, the
Aviation Act, the Pipeline Act and others; the last example is the Product Liability Act,[8]
which is a copy of the European Directive and therefore even excludes some categories
of damage to property from its coverage. In the more recent legislation, the tendency is
however to mention 'damage' without express restrictions. In these cases, it is not always
clear if the general formula is really meant to include all types of damage; still there are
also provisions which do explicitly cover certain categories of pure economic loss, such
as Art. 2 para. 1 of the Act on Liability in the field of Nuclear Energy,[9] which in letter
c) expressly mentions 'damage resulting of measures taken or recommended by *the*
authorities in *order to prevent or to reduce* an imminent nuclear danger, *except loss of
profit*'.[10]

In all these cases where implicit or explicit restrictions are established as to the types
of compensable damage, the legislator indirectly also fixes the borderline of protection
granted to individual interests by the legal order; in doing so, he simultaneously and
consistently determines the contiguous spheres of 'lawfulness' and 'unlawfulness'.

## II. Theoretical Background

*A. Description of the Problem and of the Prevailing Opinion*

Among the conditions of liability, 'unlawfulness' is probably the one that gives rise to
the most numerous and most controversial theoretical discussions while its practical
impact is – up to now[11] – very modest.

As a matter of fact, 'unlawfulness' constitutes a problem only in those cases that
can be resumed under the notion of 'pure economic loss'. In other words: if personal
injury (physical harm or a violation of 'immaterial' rights of personality, e.g., privacy,
credit etc.) or damage to property is at stake, the condition of 'unlawfulness' is
automatically considered to be fulfilled. This situation can also be defined by saying that
an interference with so-called 'absolute rights' (or: absolutely protected rights) entails
*ipso iure* an unlawful attempt on the victim's protected sphere – or at least indicates such
an attempt, subject to eventually existing 'causes of justification'. On the other hand, an
interference with (purely) economic interests of a person which is not the immediate
consequence of an attempt on absolutely protected rights will not be qualified as
'unlawful' as long as no specific norm (*'Schutznorm'*) can be found which protects

---

8    Produktehaftpflichtgesetz/Loi sur la responsabilité du fait des produits (SR/RS 221.112.944).
9    Kernenergiehaftpflichtgesetz/Loi sur la responsabilité civile en matière nucléaire (SR/RS 732.44)
10   *See* DFC 116 [1990] II 480 ff. (*supra* fn. 2 *in fine*), c.4/5 p.490 f.
11   This situation could change if the tendency to extend liability for false information and/or breach
     of trust continues to strengthen (*see infra*, item B.3.b.).

pecuniary interests precisely and accurately against interferences of the type under discussion. This view can also be expressed by saying that the assets (*'das Vermögen'*, *'la fortune'*, *'il patrimonio'*) of a person as such do not constitute an interest or position protected *in se et per se* by the Swiss legal order.[12]

It has to be stressed that this conception of 'unlawfulness', even being a quasi unanimously adopted approach,[13] is a purely doctrinal achievement which has no clear-cut base in the legal text. The reason mostly given for the assumption of the German conception in a system modelled on the French general clause is essentially a political and not a juridical one: the aim is to 'avoid an uncontrolled and uncontrollable expansion of liability', to 'keep liability in reasonable limits', to 'keep the floodgates shut' as well as possible. It is in particular alleged that, without the barrier of 'unlawfulness', the principle *'neminem laedere'* would result in unbearable impediments in daily life, especially in the field of economic competition on which liberal systems and market-economy are based and in the frame of which it must be 'lawful' to pursue one's own interests to the detriment of one's competitor[14] – at least as long as this competition is not altered by unfair or fraudulent means.

Sometimes, more or less convincing arguments are brought forward to create some appearance of scientific support for the described political choice. One of these arguments is deduced from Art. 45 SCO which specifies the heads of compensation owed in case of death and which, in para. 3, states a right to compensation in favour of those persons who, as a consequence of the death, have lost maintenance (*'Versorgerschaden'*, *'réparation pour perte de soutien'*):

> Art. 45   3. Where, as a consequence of the death, persons have lost their support, the damage resulting therefrom has *also* to be compensated.

This provision is generally considered to represent an express exception to the principle that only persons who have suffered damage as a consequence of a direct attempt to their own (absolutely protected) rights can claim for compensation; those who sustain only a 'mediate' prejudice, a so-called 'damage by ricochet' or 'reflexive damage', are normally precluded from compensation.[15]

On the same line lies the argument opposing absolute to relative, i.e., contractual rights, and concluding that an interference in a contractual relationship to which the

---

12   Oftinger/Stark, *Schweiz. Haftpflichtrecht,* Bd.I (*op.cit.* fn.2), § 4, No. 30, p. 177 f.: 'Das Vermögen ist kein Rechtsgut'. Rey, *Ausservertragliches Haftpflichtrecht,* (*op. cit.* fn.2), § 6, No. 703 – 04, p. 139 ff.; Honsell, *Schweiz. Haftpflichtrecht* (2nd ed. 1997), Zürich, § 4, No. 20, p. 46 f. *See* also DFC 118 [1992] Ib 473 ff., c.2 p.476 f., 119 [1993] II 127 ff., c.3 p. 128 ff.

13   It is true that, quite recently, this unanimity seemed somewhat to crumble; *see* in particular Werro, 'Tort liability for pure economic loss – A critique of current trends in Swiss law'; and 'Die Sorgfaltspflichtverletzung als Haftungsgrund nach Art.41 OR', (*op. cit. supra* fn.6).

14   *See* Oftinger/Stark, *Schweiz. Haftpflichtrecht,* Bd.I (*op. cit.* fn.2), § 4, No. 3 ff., p. 167 f.; *idem, Schweiz. Haftpflichtrecht,* Bd.II/1 (*op. cit.* fn.4), No. 65 ff., p. 25 ff.

15   Oftinger/Stark, *Schweiz. Haftpflichtrecht,* Bd.II/1 (*op. cit.* fn. 4), No. 96, p.34; Rey, *Ausservertragliches Haftpflichtrecht,* (*op. cit.* fn.2), § 4, No. 354 ff., p. 71 ff.

tortfeasor is not a party, is not unlawful, because there is no general legal duty to respect other people's contracts or not to interfere with them.[16] In such cases, a liability could only arise under para. 2 of Art.41 COS, based on a violation of *bonos mores,* where there was an intention to cause damage.

Still in the same direction goes the assumption that there is no general legal duty to protect other people's interests as long as these interests have not been exposed to a special risk by the person who's duty to give assistance is under discussion.[17]

## B. Theoretical Currents and Controversies

### 1. Objective and Subjective Theory

The Swiss Federal Court declares itself for the so-called 'objective theory of unlawfulness'. That means that a fact causing damage is 'unlawful' if

'it constitutes a violation of a general legal duty, be it that it interferes with an absolute right of the injured person (*Erfolgsunrecht*), be it that a pure economic loss results from the violation of a pertinent protective norm (*Verhaltensunrecht*). Unlawfulness lies in the objective infringement of a norm and is cancelled where a cause of justification is given.'[18]

This 'objective theory' is opposed to the so-called 'subjective theory' according to which each damage (or fact causing damage) is 'unlawful' unless the tortfeasor can invoke a special and legally founded authorisation that procures him a subjective justification to cause damage to another person.[19]

The difference between these two theories is more one of philosophical and dogmatical perspectives than of effective practical importance. The objective theory proceeds from the principle that 'everything which is not expressly prohibited, is allowed',[20] while the subjective theory starts from the opposite concept.

These different approaches could have consequences under the aspect of evidence: one could argue that, under the objective theory, the person claiming compensation has to prove that the damage he suffered was caused 'unlawfully', whereas, under the

---

16   Oftinger/Stark, *Schweiz. Haftpflichtrecht,* Bd.II/1 (*op. cit.* fn.4), No. 202 ff., p. 65 f.; *idem, Schweiz. Haftpflichtrecht,* Bd.I (*op. cit.* fn.2), No. 32 ff. p. 178 f; Rey, *Ausservertragliches Haftpflichtrecht,* (*op. cit.* fn.2), § 6, No. 665 ff., p. 132 ff. (part.: No. 713 ff, p. 141 f.). *See* also DFC 114 [1988] II 97 ff.

17   Brehm, *Berner Kommentar,* (Kommentar zum schweizerischen Privatrecht), Bd. VI/1/3 (1986-1990), Bern, No. 56 ad Art.41 COS; *see* also DFC 115 [1989] II 15 ff.; Oftinger/Stark, *Schweiz. Haftpflichtrecht,* Bd.I (*op. cit.* fn. 2), § 3, No. 60, p. 128 f.

18   DFC 115 [1989] II 15 ff.; *see* also DFC 121 [1995] III 350 ff; 120 [1994] II 331 ff; 118 [1992] Ib 473 ff.

19   *See* Oftinger/Stark, *Schweiz. Haftpflichtrecht,* Bd.I (*op. cit.* fn. 2), § 4, No. 9 ff., p.169 ff.; Rey, *Ausservertragliches Haftpflichtrecht,* (*op. cit.* fn. 2), No. 670 f., p. 133 f.

20   DFC 106 [1980] IV 136 ff. (c.6, p. 141): 'In der Schweiz gilt, dass gestattet ist, was nicht ausdrücklich verboten wurde'.

subjective theory, the tortfeasor would have to prove that he had a sufficient cause of justification. We don't think this conclusion is correct,[21] simply because 'unlawfulness' – being a value judgement and not a fact – is not a proper item to be proved. Evidence can only be given on facts and acts which will then have to be qualified as 'lawful' or 'unlawful' by the judge.

What may be retained as a conclusion from the two opposite theories, is the impression that the objective theory is more likely to achieve the restrictive influence which the element of 'unlawfulness' is supposed to exert on liability, than would the subjective theory which tends on the contrary to enlarge the field of damage caused '*non iure*'. It is equally true, however, that the advocates of the (more restrictive) objective theory are frequently obliged, in order to reach socially adequate results, to invent new norms, creating new types of legally protected interests and/or new duties or prohibitions, the violation of which can entail liability.[22] And *vice versa* the supporters of the subjective theory will constantly have to accept new grounds of justification, if they want to keep liability within reasonable limits.

## 2. Wrongfulness of the Result or of the Act?
A more interesting and significant distinction is that made between the 'wrongfulness of the result' (*Erfolgsunrecht*) and the 'wrongfulness of the conduct' (*Verhaltensunrecht*).

In a short essay[23] which is still the leading doctrinal statement on 'unlawfulness' in Swiss law – in spite also of the fact that during the forty years elapsed since its publication a great number of new dissertations on this subject have appeared[24] – Merz has shown that there are essentially two categories with reference to which '*Widerrechtlichkeit*' as a condition of liability can be established:

(1) an infringement on a legally and absolutely (*erga omnes*) protected right ('*absolut geschütztes Rechtsgut*'), in particular the right of personality (including physical and psychical integrity) and real rights (property, possession);

and, if no absolutely protected right is affected:

(2) an infringement upon a norm of conduct (precept or prohibition) aiming precisely at the protection of one's assets against precisely that type of attempt, independently from any interference with the bodily integrity of the victim or its material goods.

Where 'unlawfulness' is determined by reference to an absolutely protected legal position, it is the result (*Erfolg*) of the interference that 'is unlawful' in itself. Where, on

---

21  *See* in the same sense, but with a different reasoning: DFC 115 [1989] II 15 ff., in part. c.3b, p. 19 f.

22  Gauch, *Grundbegriffe des ausservertraglichen Haftungsrechts*, (*op. cit.* fn.2), p. 232 f.

23  'Die Widerrechtlichkeit gemäss Art. 41 OR als Rechtsquellenproblem', in ZBJV (*Zeitschrift des Bernischen Juristenvereins*) 91bis [1955]: *Festgabe für den Schweizerischen Juristenverein, Rechtsquellenprobleme im schweizerischen Recht,* p. 301 ff.

24  *See* Oftinger/Stark, *Schweiz. Haftpflichtrecht*, Bd.I (*op. cit.* fn. 2), § 4, p. 165 (bibliography).

the other hand, no such position can be found – i.e., where pecuniary losses do not derive from any personal injury or damage to things – only the way in which the tortfeasor has acted, his behaviour (*Verhalten*), is susceptible of being qualified as contravening a specific norm with a specific protective purpose (*'Schutzzweck'*).

The distinction looks very clear. Yet, it is not as easy to handle as it would seem. The problem lies in the circumstance that, on the one hand, not all rights and legal positions which are supposed to deserve absolute protection are defined and delimited (like, e.g., corporal integrity) in a way sufficiently sharp to allow their violation to be ascertained without any doubt. This difficulty can be illustrated by taking as an example the right to privacy which is indisputably an 'absolute right'; its borderline can nevertheless be very delicate to draw. The right to privacy of a politician during his campaign for election is not necessarily the same as anybody else's right to privacy.[25] Similarly, the right of property (which is often considered to be the most sacrosanct and inviolable right of all) may not be as clear-cut as that, where one has to determine whether an emission from neighbouring ground is excessive or has to be tolerated.

Yet, wherever a position is considered to be worth of legal protection, this automatically means that there must also exist a norm aiming at its protection. Conversely, wherever one admits the existence of a norm intended to protect patrimonial interests against a determined type of attempt, this inevitably means the recognition of a corresponding (and insofar absolutely protected) right, like, e.g., the 'right of the enterprise set up and actually run' (*'Recht am eingerichteten und ausgeübten Gewerbebetrieb'*) or a 'right to fair competition' or even a 'right to loyalty' (in the sense of a 'right to be treated according to the principle of good faith'[26]).

In other words, the two above-mentioned categories are of a complementary character (as are unlawfulness and justification), representing two sides of the same coin; they are therefore not very helpful in solving the problem of where to draw the borderline between 'lawfulness' and 'unlawfulness' – whether it be in general or in a specific doubtful case.

However, coming back to the distinction between unlawful result and unlawful conduct and looking at it from a general point of view, it seems correct to say that the approach referring rather to the result, than to the act which caused that result, fits better with civil liability (in contrast, perhaps, to criminal law), because tort law comes actually into play only where damage has effectively occurred, i.e., where the prejudice is done. A behaviour can, indeed, be ever so reprehensible and can violate as many norms as one can imagine – if it entails no economically measurable loss (immaterial prejudice as pain and suffering being here left aside), it remains irrelevant under the aspect of civil liability. That is why tort law must naturally concentrate on the 'unlawfulness of the result'.

---

25  Oftinger/Stark, *Schweiz. Haftpflichtrecht,* Bd.II/1 (*op. cit.* fn. 4), No. 47 ff., p. 19 ff. *See* also Tercier, *Le nouveau droit de la personalité* (1984), Zürich, § 8 ff., p. 79 ff.; and, recently, Portmann, 'Erfolgsunrecht oder Verhaltensunrecht? Zugleich ein Beitrag zur Abgrenzung von Widerrechtlichkeit und Verschulden im Haftpflichtrecht', in: SJZ [*Schweizerische Juristen-Zeitung*] 93 [1997], 273 ff., who takes the trouble to delimit the right of privacy as an argument to repudiate *in toto* the theory of 'wrongfulness of the result', (dis-) qualifying it at the same time as antiquated.
26  *See infra*, item II.B.3 under (b).

Moreover, this is the only way in which one can explain why unlawfulness is also required in the field of strict liability, where the essential connecting fact is not the individual conduct of a tortfeasor, but a certain legally defined risk situation.[27] To focus on the result is also the only way by which it is possible to draw a clear distinction between 'unlawfulness' as a general and objective condition of liability on the one hand, and 'fault' on the other hand, which is the subjective criterion that makes it possible to impute the damage to a given individual, to shift the loss from the person who suffered it directly to that other person who is made responsible.

In fact, where liability is connected to human behaviour, it becomes fairly difficult to distinguish 'unlawfulness' (sometimes called the 'objective aspect of fault') from 'fault' (which could also be defined as 'the subjective aspect of unlawfulness').[28] The same question is then examined twice under different viewpoints, or rather: the evaluation of fault is narrowed down to the mere question of imputability in the sense of the mental capacity of the wrongdoer to understand and control his acts (discernment). In this way, the approach which refers 'unlawfulness' to the act contributes to the so-called 'objectivation' of the concept of fault and to blur the distinction between liability for fault (negligence) and strict liability.[29]

## 3. The Norm and its Protective Aim

It is generally recognized that the rules, the violation of which entails the (dis-)qualification of an infringement on somebody's interests as 'unlawful', can be found everywhere within the legal order; that is to say: not only in the main (civil) code, but in any other act, be it in the field of private, criminal or administrative law, and on the federal as well as on the cantonal level, or in the statutes of a municipality; moreover, unlawfulness can be deduced from the infringement of unwritten rules, of general principles of law. In some cases, courts have even referred to soft law (e.g., directives of the

---

27  *See supra* fn. 2.

28  This difficulty may partly explain why Article 1382 of the French civil code, which is obviously the model that has inspired art.41 COS, simply ignores the distinction. This is also the problem which Portmann, 'Erfolgsunrecht oder Verhaltensunrecht?' (*op. cit.* fn. 25) is unable to solve under his approach of exclusive 'wrongfulness of behaviour' which leads inevitably to a confusion between wrongfulness and fault; his 'Beitrag zur Abgrenzung von Widerrechtlichkeit und Verschulden im Haftpflichtrecht' can therefore not really be considered as a very successful one. It is again the same reason that makes Werro, 'Tort liability for pure economic loss – A critique of current trends in Swiss law' and 'Die Sorgfaltspflichtverletzung als Haftungsgrund nach Art. 41 OR', (*op. cit. supra* fn. 6) coming up with a concept in which wrongfulness and negligence are melted into one another, a concept that practically amounts to the French notion of '*faute*'. In the same sense: Schwenzer and Schönenberger, 'Civil Liability for Purely Economic Loss in Switzerland', in *Swiss Reports presented at the XVth International Congress of Comparative Law (Bristol 1998)* (1998), Publications of the Swiss Institute of Comparative Law No.33, Zürich, p. 353 ff.

29  Oftinger/Stark, *Schweiz. Haftpflichtrecht*, Bd.I (*op. cit.* fn. 2), § 4, No. 50 ff., p. 184 ff.; Widmer, 'Gefahren des Gefahrensatzes', in ZBJV (*op. cit.* fn. 23) 106 [1970] p. 289 ff. (in part.: p. 305 ff.).

Institute for research in snow and avalanche, rules of football or skiing federations, codes of professional conduct like the directives of the Academy of Medical Sciences etc.) [30]

(a) Problems arise in particular where the norm referred to is either formulated in a very sharp and narrow way (like some traffic rules: e.g., the prescription to drive on the right or – as in England and Japan – on the left side of the road) or, on the contrary, where very general and undetermined norms are brought into the picture. In the first case, the difficulty lies in clarifying if this specific rule was really intended to protect this specific interest. This is the question frequently addressed as the 'relation of unlawfulness' (*Widerrechtlichkeitszusammenhang*) or '(aim of the norm) *Normzweck*'. This concept proceeds from the idea that it is not sufficient, when ascertaining the unlawfulness of an attempt on somebody's rights, to identify a norm that has been infringed as such; in an additional step, one has to make sure that the violated rule was really meant to protect this specific (economic) interest.

The problem is especially well perceptible in the so-called 'cable cases'. Under a strict régime of unlawfulness, where purely economical interests would be protected only in exceptional cases, on the basis of a clear norm, clients suffering damage as a consequence of the rupture in supply with energy or water would normally not be entitled to bring an action against the author of the rupture, unless they were themselves the owners of the interrupted cable or pipe. In its recent jurisprudence, however, the Federal Court has loosened these restrictions and has adjudicated compensation by applying a provision of the Criminal code which makes it an offence to disturb or impair enterprises of public interest.[31] The novelty in this approach was that the Court considered the provision to protect not only public interests but also those of individual persons or enterprises who were dependant upon the products supplied by such public enterprises. And it is very significant to note that in the reasons given by the Court for its decision, it says that it does not matter whether the problem is examined under the aspect of unlawfulness or under the aspect of (adequate) causation.[32] This consideration confirms the impression that the concept of '*Normzweck*' as well as doctrines like those of 'relevant', 'proximate' or 'adequate' causality are only different expressions for one and the same problem: that of determining the range of application of a given liability, or, in other words and focusing more on the persons concerned: the question how to define the sphere of risk of each of them.

(b) The problem is posed the other way round where unlawfulness is deduced from very vague and general rules, whether written or unwritten. As far as written principles are concerned, one very actual question is to clarify if and to what extent the principle of

---

30   Oftinger/Stark, *Schweiz. Haftpflichtrecht,* Bd.I (*op. cit.* fn. 2), § 4, No. 42/43f., p. 182; A. Keller, *Haftpflicht im Privatrecht,* (5th ed. 1993), Bern, p. 91 f.
31   Art. 239 of the Swiss Criminal Code (SCrimC; Strafgesetzbuch/Code pénal, SR/RS 31 1. 0).
32   DFC 101 [1975] Ib 252 ff.: 102 [1976] II 85 ff.; on the contrary: DFC 106 [1980] II 75 ff. (*see supra* fn. 7); a parallel reasoning was however refused in respect of art. 229 SCrimC (Violation of rules of good architectural practice): DFC 117 [1991] II 259 ff. and 119 [1993] II 127 ff.

good faith – laid down in Art. 2 of the Swiss Civil code – can be used as an autonomous protective norm in order to establish liability. A series of decisions of the Federal Court, already classified under the label 'Vertrauenshaftung' (= liability for breach of trust),[33] indicate that in this sector, too, things are moving. In the most recent of these cases, the Federal Court approved the claim of a sportsman against his federation for compensation of earnings he had lost by participating in different training camps; he had accepted these losses in view of his expected selection for the World Championship, an expectation which had subsequently been frustrated by an adverse and unfair decision of the federation.[34] In its decision the Court gave a good synopsis of the evolution of its jurisprudence showing its increasing willingness to assume – even outside contractual links – certain special relationships on the basis of which partners may rely upon fair and loyal conduct towards each other and may, if this faith is frustrated, claim compensation for misguided investments and pointless expenses.

In a former case, a holding company has been held liable for misleading advertisement of one of its affiliated societies *vis-à-vis* a third party.[35] This judgment has itself to be seen in the prolongation of other decisions which accepted liability for economic loss due to false or incorrect information provided by someone who could be considered to be a specialist in the relevant matter.[36] And if one wishes to go even further in retracing the lineage of this jurisprudence, one will come across the cases based on so-called '*culpa in contrahendo*'; this was so to say the first backdoor through which the principle of good faith was allowed to escape from the enclosure of privity of contract.[37] Today it seems realistic to assume that a new variety of liability based on 'breach of trust', derived from the general principle of good faith, will continue to develop, and that the move could even increase further.[38]

---

33   A. K. Schnyder, *Basler Kommentar zum Schweizerischen Privatrecht*, Obligationenrecht I (2nd ed. 1996), Basel/Frankfurt a.M., No. 36 and 44. ad Art. 41 SCO; Walter, 'Vertrauenshaftung im Umfeld des Vertrages', in: ZBJV (*op. cit.* fn. 23) 132 [1996] 273 ff.; Wick, 'Die Vertrauenshaftung im schweizerischen Recht' in: AJP (*Aktuelle Juristische Praxis*) 10/95, 1270 ff. (ad DFC 120 [1990] II 331 ff., *infra* fn. 35).

34   DFC 121 [1995] III 350 ff.

35   DFC 120 [1994] II 331 ff.; *see* also Fellmann, 'Haftung für Werbung – ein erster Schritt zu einer allgemeinen Vertrauenshaftung?', in: *medialex* (*Revue de droit de la communication/Zeitschrift für Kommunikationsrecht*) 2/95, 94 ff.

36   DFC 112 [1986] II 347; 111 [1985] II 347. *See* also Rey, *Ausservertragliches Haftpflichtrecht*, (*op. cit.* fn. 2), No. 721 E, p. 143; Honsell, *Schweiz. Haftpflichtrecht*, (*op. cit.*, fn. 12), § 4 No. 22-24, p. 47 f.

37   *See* Merz, *Vertrag und Vertragsschluss* (2nd ed. 1992), Fribourg, § 3, p. 69 ff.; A. Koller, *Schweiz. Obligationenrecht*, Bd.I Allgemeiner Teil (1996), Bern, § 28, p. 408 ff.

38   This evolution had been prepared for a fairly long time by several authors, in particular Peter Jäggi, Jean-Michel Grossen, Max Keller, Walter Schluep and Heinz Rey (*see* the references given by this last author in: *Ausservertragliches Haftpflichtrecht*, (*op. cit.* fn. 21), No. 717 ff., p. 142 f. and No. 741 ff, p. 146 ff); in the same sense: Widmer, 'Variationen über Treu und Glauben', in: Schluep (ed.), *Recht, Staat und Politik am Ende des zweiten Jahrtausends, Festschrift zum 60. Geburtstag von Bundesrat Prof. Arnold Koller* (1993), Bern/Stuttgart/Wien, p. 185 ff., in part. ch.V, p. 198 ff.

(c) Among the unwritten rules that may be used (or misused) in order to establish unlawfulness of a fact having caused (pure economic) damage, we have finally to mention the so-called '*Gefahrensatz*' (=principle of provoked danger).[39] This rule which has also been called a 'fundamental principle of the legal order',[40] is simply another way to express the roman adage '*neminem laedere*', i.e., exactly the excessively vague maxim which the criterion of unlawfulness is supposed to confine. The real significance of this rule (which is something like the Swiss version of the German '*Verkehrssicherung-pflicht*' and of the 'duty of care' known to common law systems) has been very well explained in a decision of the Federal Court going back to 1938;[41] this text states very clearly that a duty to take adequate safety measures in order to avoid damage is imposed (only) on the person who has created or who maintains a situation of *unnecessary* risk; the 'fundamental principle' is therefore exclusively related to the question of fault, and more precisely to that type of fault or negligence which consists in assuming a risk without possessing the necessary capacities to control it ('*Übernahmeverschulden*'). Where, on the contrary, the rule is taken as a norm allowing the establishment of the 'unlawfulness' of the risky conduct, it will lead to absurd consequences as happened in a case where the Federal Court declared that skiing was lawful only as long as the skier did not expose anybody else to a danger of being hurt.[42] This is precisely the same reasoning as that used by the *Münchner Oberlandesgericht* in a famous decision in 1861 where it held that 'running a railway using locomotive engines constitutes necessarily and inevitably a negligent conduct...'.[43] Applied generally, such a view would enable the judge to consider automatically every imaginable damage to be unlawful and to result from negligence, because each attempt can retrospectively be related to a pre-existing situation of risk that has obviously not been sufficiently secured by preventive measures.[44]

Nowadays, this opinion is abandoned and the Federal Court follows the predominant opinion according to which the '*Gefahrensatz*' is not a universal stopgap in the case of missing protective norms with a concrete substance.[45]

---

39  *See* Widmer (*op. cit.* fn. 29); Rey, *Ausservertragliches Haftpflichtrecht,* (*op. cit.* fn. 2), No. 753 ff., p. 148, Oftinger/Stark, *Schweiz. Haftpflichtrecht,* Bd.I (*op. cit.* fn. 2), § 3, No. 54 ff., p. 127 ff.; *ibidem,* § 4, No. 44, p. 182 f.; Oftinger/Stark, *Schweiz. Haftpflichtrecht,* Bd.II/1 (*op. cit.* fn. 4), § 16, No. 26 ff., p. 11 ff. and No. 107, p. 39.
40  Oftinger, *Schweiz Haftpflichtrecht,* Bd. I (4th ed. 1975), Zürich, § 3/III/D, p. 88.
41  DFC 64 [1938] II 254 ff.
42  DFC 82 [1956] II 28 ff. It is not by chance, therefore, that authors who tend to merge unlawfulness and fault, like to refer to this decision: Werro, 'Die Sorgfaltspflichtverletzung als Haftungsgrund nach Art.41 OR', (*op. cit. supra* fn. 6), p. 348 f.
43  Seuffert's Archiv 14 [1861] Nr. 208, p. 354 ff.
44  Widmer, 'Gefahren des Gefahrensatzes', (*op. cit.* fn. 29).
45  BGE 119 [1993] II 127 ff. (c.3, p. 129 *in fine*).

## III. 'Unlawfulness' in the Actual Reform Project of Swiss Tort Law

According to the preliminary draft of a 'General Part of Swiss Tort Law' (DGP) 'unlawfulness' should continue to fulfil its function as a creative and at the same time restrictive element, requirement or general condition of liability. In this sense, it appears from the very first provision of the draft, the 'basic norm of imputation', which reads as follows:

| | |
|---|---|
| *A. Fundamental rule* *of imputation* | **Art. 1.** A person is liable for compensation of the damage caused to another person insofar as the fact causing the damage can be imputed to him by virtue of the law. 2. Damage *unlawfully* caused can be imputed in particular: 1. to the person whose behaviour has caused it and who is at fault (Art. 17); 2. to the person availing himself of the services of one or more agents (Art.20 and 21); 3. to the person who operates a particularly dangerous activity (Art. 22). |

Subsequently, 'unlawfulness' is set out as the second general condition of liability (after damage) and it is specified that it acquires a particular connotation when applied to liability connected with human conduct, i.e., liability based on fault:

| | |
|---|---|
| *II. Unlawfulness* *1. Definition* | **Art. 13** 1. A fact causing damage is *unlawful* when it impinges on a right protected by the legal order. 2. Where the fact causing damage consists in the behaviour of a person (Art. 17-19), *this behaviour is unlawful* when it is contrary to a duty or a prohibition imposed by the legal order, to the principle of good faith or to a contractual duty. |

Before that, the problem is already addressed under another heading, namely that of 'damage':

| | |
|---|---|
| *C. General conditions* *I. Damage* | **Art.6** *1. Damage includes pecuniary loss as well as pain and suffering* 2. Pecuniary loss includes the categories mentioned in the following Articles 7 – 10 and pure economic loss. |
| *1. Types of damage* | 3. Subject to contrary provisions, compensation based on liability for risk can only be awarded for damage resulting from an attempt to life or to physical or psychical integrity of a person, to physical objects or to the environment. |

The idea is to resume the actual position as it results from jurisprudence and from the state of legal science. There is no ambition whatsoever to solve definitely the problem, in particular with regard to 'pure economic losses', an enterprise which – by the way – could turn out to be as difficult as the squaring of the circle or the construction of a *perpetuum mobile*. The only and somewhat timid attempt to cut the Gordian knot is the provision of Art. 6 para. 3 DGP which excludes in principle pure economic loss from the compensable damage under strict liability. In doing so, it generalizes the rule contained in different special acts[46] and which can be explained in a rather convincing way by arguing that the aim of those provisions which establish a strict liability is precisely and exclusively to protect persons, property and environment from physical danger inherent in modern technology. Damage which is not an immediate consequence of such 'lawfully' created technical risks should accordingly be compensated only where a fault has been committed; in this case, 'unlawfulness of the conduct' may also be found in the violation of the principle of good faith or in the breach of a contractual duty.

---

46  *See supra* item I.B

# Conclusions

Helmut Koziol

## I. Preliminary Observations

The reports show that 'wrongfulness' plays a decisive role in establishing liability under the law of every country. In the area of liability based on fault, the tortfeasor can only be held responsible for the damage if his behaviour was incorrect. But 'wrongfulness' has quite different meanings under the respective legal systems. The result of these differences for example is that in some countries wrongfulness is only of importance in the area of liability based on fault, but in Switzerland also in the field of strict liability.[1] However, even under those legal systems which refer to wrongfulness only in the area of liability based on fault, the meaning of wrongfulness differs strongly. Whereas under some systems the result is qualified as wrongful (*'Erfolgsunrechtslehre'*), under other systems the behaviour of the tortfeasor has to be wrongful (*'Verhaltensunrechtslehre'*).[2] For example, the first is true under Swiss law[3] and, according to the dominant opinion,[4] also in Germany as far as *'unmittelbare Eingriffe'* (direct interference) in absolute rights are at stake. But some German scholars emphasize that even if the result is decisive the behaviour has to be judged.[5] Dutch law[6] explicitly relates to the act. Likewise, that the behaviour has to be qualified is the general opinion under Austrian law[7] as well as under Greek[8] and South African[9] law and this theory corresponds also to the breach of standard of care under English law.[10] As French lawyers do not strictly keep fault and wrongful-

---

1    *Cf.* Widmer's report I.A.
2    *Cf.* the reports on Case 13.
3    *Cf.* Widmer's report II.B.2. and Art. 1 sec. 2 of the new draft on liability.
4    Von Caemmerer, *Wandlungen des Deliktsrechts, Festschrift zum 100jährigen Bestehen des deutschen Juristentages II* (1960), p. 75 ff.; Stoll, 'Unrechtstypen bei Verletzung absoluter Rechte', *Archiv für die civilistische Praxis* (AcP) 162, 1963, 203; Deutsch, *Fahrlässigkeit und erforderliche Sorgfalt* (2nd ed. 1995), p. 229 f., 282.
5    *Cf.* Münzberg, *Verhalten und Erfolg als Grundlagen der Rechtswidrigkeit und Haftung* (1966); Brüggemeier, *Deliktsrecht* (1986), No. 95; Kötz, *Deliktsrecht* (7th ed. 1996), No. 98 ff. *See* also Larenz and Canaris, *Lehrbuch des Schuldrechts,* II/2: Besonderer Teil (13th ed. 1994), § 75 II 3.
6    Art 6:162 BW, *cf.* the report by Spier section I.
7    Austrian report I.C.1.
8    *See* the report by Kerameus section I.4.
9    *Cf.* Neethling section I.
10   *See* the English report under 'General'.

*H. Koziol (ed.), Unification of Tort Law: Wrongfulness*, 129–135.
©1998 *Kluwer Law International. Printed in The Netherlands.*

ness separately[11] one has to assume that they also qualify the behaviour and not the result; the same seems to be true under Belgian law.[12] To some extent Italian law tries to synthesize both ways of establishing wrongfulness.[13]

But there are further differences, e.g., the borderline between objective 'wrongfulness' and subjective 'fault' is drawn very clearly under some legal systems,[14] whereas under others hardly any distinction is made.[15] Under Dutch law opinions are strongly divided.[16] German lawyers certainly distinguish between wrongfulness and fault, but as they use an objective yardstick in checking fault the distinction is of minor importance.[17]

As the concepts and the functions of wrongfulness under the different legal systems are various and there are good reasons for every view taken, the majority of the members of the Tilburg Group is of the opinion that we have to try, to some extent, to take into consideration all of them and to integrate as far as reasonable the view of all legal systems.

## II. The Method of Proceeding in Establishing Wrongfulness

We believe – at least at this stage of the discussion – that the best way to reach this goal is to approach the question of whether misconduct of the tortfeasor is given or not, by referring to the following steps:

1.   The first decisive step is to decide whether the actor violated an imperative rule which forbids a certain conduct or whether he endangered rights and interests which the legal system is intended to protect to a greater or lesser extent. In doing so, the actor caused a result which – in a very general, abstract sense – the legal system is designed to prohibit.[18] This examination corresponds, on the whole, to that carried out according to the '*Erfolgsunrechtslehre*': unlawfulness is accepted only because of interference with protected interests and, therefore, due solely to the unwanted result. The duty of care concept in English law straddles this step as the duty of care is primarily important as a mechanism for identifying the interests protected by law and the extent of their protection.

If the actor neither violated a rule requiring a certain behaviour nor interfered with protected interests, there can be no liability based on fault. Even if the conditions for one of these hypotheses are met, that alone is not sufficient to establish liability based on fault. Still, this first question is important in order to determine the nature of the grounds for taking action to restrain interference and to establish whether the person whose

---

11   French report section I.A.
12   *Cf.* Cousy's report section I.
13   Italian report section I.
14   *Cf.* the report under Austrian law section I.D.
15   *See* Viney's report section I.A.
16   *Cf.* Spier's report section III. and IV.
17   In detail Deutsch, *Fahrlässigkeit und erforderliche Sorgfalt* (2nd ed. 1995), p. 137 ff., p. 299 ff., p. 476 f. *Cf.* also the Greek report section I.3.b.
18   *Cf.* Larenz and Canaris, *Lehrbuch des Schuldrechts,* II/2, § 75 II 3.

interests are endangered has the right to self-defence: if protected interests are endangered and, consequently, the very abstract legal elements of a tort are given, the person whose interests are endangered has the right to repulse the attack.[19] Furthermore, the second prerequisite of liability, namely the breach of a duty of care, may be indicated if the defendant interfered with protected interests.[20]

2. The second step, which is not decisive in the area of strict liability, is to examine in a more concrete way whether, under the circumstances, the actor violated the general, objective standard of care, which has to be determined by considering various factors. This step largely corresponds to the theory of unlawfulness of conduct ('*Verhaltensunrechtslehre*') under civil law and also to that of breach of standard of care under English law.

It is on the agenda whether this second step only is decisive in the area of interference with protected interests or also if the tortfeasor violated an imperative rule.[21] I think the latter is true: even if the injurer violated an imperative rule he cannot be reproached for his behaviour if he behaved as carefully as a reasonable man was able to do. Therefore, the situation is exactly the same as in the case of interference with protected rights.

3. In the third and final step, the questions at stake are of whether liability depends on subjective fault and whether the specific injurer can be blamed considering his subjective conditions. The questions whether subjective fault is decisive or whether a violation of the objective standard of care is sufficient and also how relevant subjective fault is still have to be discussed separately in greater detail.

The following has to be stressed: laying down the stated conditions for liability based on fault still does not mean that the tortfeasor is liable provided that these conditions are given for every single damage or part of damage. The question of whether the inquiry for wrongfulness only applies to the 'initial damage' and liability is thus established for consequential damage as well or whether wrongfulness has to be verified in regard to every part of damage has to be discussed separately, be it in connection with causation or the protective purpose of the norm or other factors relevant in establishing liability.

## III. Protected Rights and Interests

If the legal system recognizes protected positions of a person, then it demands that all others respect those rights and interests to a reasonable extent. The owner of the protected

---

19 In this spirit in Germany Larenz and Canaris, *Lehrbuch des Schuldrechts*, II/2, § 75 II 3.
20 *See* the Swiss report sec. II.A.; the Austrian report sec. I.C.1. Under German law *cf.* again Larenz and Canaris, *Lehrbuch des Schuldrechtts*, II/2, § 75 II 3 c.
21 *Cf.* Cousy, report section III; Widmer, report section II.B.2.; report under Austrian law section I.C.1. Under German law *cf.* Esser and Weyers, *Schuldrecht*, II: Besonderer Teil (7th ed. 1991), § 56 I.

right or interest does not have to tolerate interference without justification; he has the right to apply for an injunction and the right to self-defence.

The legal system can specify the areas of protection in two ways: on the one hand, it can forbid or demand a more or less predetermined behaviour;[22] from this one may conclude that the law is intended to protect certain interests which would otherwise be endangered. On the other hand, the legal system can describe the protected rights or interests and demand in a rather general way that they not be interfered with as far as is reasonable.[23] The two methods may also be combined.

The question of how extensive the protection of an interest of a person is and, therefore, which behaviour is required from all others can be answered rather easily if there is a particular imperative rule which forbids (due to its abstract dangerousness) to endanger an interest through a conduct which is fairly precisely described. The issue becomes more difficult if the law only provides that others must not act *contra bonos mores*.

Establishing the level of protection is also more difficult if the legal system only describes the rights or interests to be protected as far as is reasonable. Then the scope of protection and the behaviour demanded from others are the point in question. In discussing the topic of finding out the level of protection, the members of the Tilburg Group came to the conclusion that the nature and the value of the interest has especially to be taken into account.[24] The fundamental rights of personality such as the rights to life, health and liberty rank highest. Rights *in rem* and intangible property rights rank slightly lower; pure economic or pure immaterial interests are at the lower end of the scale. Other important factors are the clarity of the description and the obviousness of the interest. The rights to life, liberty and also of property have reasonably clear contours and they are rather obvious. Contractual rights, it is true, have clear contours in the isolated case, but their content varies from case to case and they are also not that obvious. Pure economic and immaterial interests do not have clear contours even in the isolated case and they are by no means obvious. But one must consider not only the protected interests, but also the interest in free movement of those who have to respect them as well as public interests: the far-reaching protection of interests which are not obvious, e.g., of contractual rights and even more so of pure economic interests, would restrict everyone's freedom of movement to an unreasonable extent. Therefore, the protection of such interests has to be restricted; they are only protected against intentional actions. Furthermore, freedom of movement would also be restricted unreasonably if everyone had to reckon with practically unrestricted liability.

According to the above, the fundamental, clearly outlined rights of personality, the rights *in rem* and the intangible property rights enjoy far-reaching protection. Because

---

22  *Cf.* the reports under Austrian (sec. I.C.2), Belgian (sec. II.), Dutch (sec. I.), and Swiss law (section II.B.3.); under German law *see* § 823 sec 2 Bürgerliches Gesetzbuch (BGB, Civil Code).

23  *Cf.* the reports of Cousy section II, Neethling section I., Widmer section II.B.2., and the Austrian report section I.C.2.

24  *Cf.* Neethling, section II.; Austrian report section I.C.3. and the additional Austrian report on 'The Nature of the Interests Protected by Tort Law'. In the same sense Schilcher and Posch, 'Civil Liability for Pure Economic Loss: An Austrian Perspective', in: Banakas (ed.), *Civil Liability for Pure Economic Loss* (1996), p. 174 ff. Under German law *see* Möllers, *Rechtsgüterschutz im Umwelt - und Haftungsrecht* (1996), p. 142 ff., p. 378 ff.

of the very special rank enjoyed by the rights of personality, even immaterial interests, e.g., not to suffer pain, are included in the protection. As to the rights of personality which do not have such clear contours, the interest of all others in the freedom of movement has to be considered. Therefore, the right to honour or reputation is protected against true comments only to a small extent.[25] Even if the comment is untrue, the right of others to free statement of opinion and the interest in full information have to be considered.[26] Regarding contractual rights, it carries weight that the interests are of lower ranking and that they have various contents and are not obvious.[27] This is even more so the case for pure economic interests, as they did not take shape in a right.[28] Therefore, the competing interests of others have to be valued as being of equal rank. As a consequence, pure economic interests, e.g., the chance to net a profit, enjoy protection only to a very limited extent.[29] Even more restricted is the protection of pure immaterial interests, e.g., not to be worried or frightened by someone's behaviour.

It has to be pointed out that the extent of protection of rights or interests depends on whether one or more of a number of factors are given, also on the weight of these factors and their combination with other factors. As the scope of protection depends on the total weight of the factors, it may, therefore, even be that a high-ranking interest enjoys no protection if opposite interests prevail,[30] e.g., if, on the one hand, the endangering of health is only very slight and, on the other hand, the actor would suffer severe damage to his property if he had to respect the right to physical well-being.

Finally, it has to be stressed that the protection of interests accepted under tort law may be intensified considerably if there is a relationship or proximity between the actor and the person whose interests are endangered.[31] For example, proximity is very strong between the partners of a contract; this can be true even prior to conclusion of said contract; a special proximity is also given between the person who is responsible for a prospectus and those persons to whom the information is addressed.

## IV. General, Objective Standard of Care

If the standard of care towards the protected interests of others is not precisely described by law, establishing the standard requires balancing the interests of the person who needs protection and those of the actor.[32] Here again it is important to consider, first of all, the value of the endangered interests and the significance of the threatening interference, on

---

25   *See* the reports on Case 6.
26   *See* the reports on Case 7.
27   *Cf.* the reports on Case 2.
28   *Cf.* the reports on Cases 1, 3 and 4.
29   *Cf.* the reports on Case 1.
30   *Cf.* the reports on Case 9.
31   *Cf.* Rogers' report on Case 10; Rogers in *Winfield & Jolowicz on Tort* (14th. ed. 1994), p. 99 and p. 104; Italian and Austrian additional reports on 'The Borderline between Tort Liability and Contract'. Furthermore the reports on Cases 11 and 12.
32   *Cf.* to this topic Rogers in *Winfield & Jolowicz on Tort* (14th ed. 1994), p. 132ff.

the one hand, and the interests pursued by the actor, on the other. Also, relevant are the aptness of the conduct to cause damage,[33] the foreseeability of the damage[34] the proximity between the endangered person and the actor, the knowledge by the actor that the endangered person would rely on his conduct, the insurability of the risk at stake,[35] the burden (costs) of avoiding endangering the protected interests and the reasonableness of such costs.[36] It should also be taken into account whether the protection demands simply the omission of a dangerous conduct or even taking positive action to prevent harm.[37]

Here are some examples which illustrate establishing a violation of the general, objective standard of care.

As to the duties of care concerning the physical well being of other persons, the high rank of this interest plays an important role. In addition, the degree of dangerousness and the significance of the menacing interference have to be considered: the duties of a skier, inline skater or cyclist to take care become stricter as their speed increases and as traffic becomes denser. Likewise, the duties of care of a person who knowingly suffers from an infectious disease become stricter as the danger of infection increases and as the interference to physical well being grows. If very significant interference to health or even a menace to life is involved, the actor may even have a duty to act positively to prevent harm, if such a duty only interferes with minor interests on his part.[38]

In regard to the protection of contractual relations, one has to consider that a position recognized by law still exists, which, however, is of lower rank than the rights of personality or the rights *in rem*. Furthermore, the content of contractual relations varies and is not obvious. Therefore, the interest of all other persons to exercise their freedom of movement would be restricted very seriously if law required them to make inquiries as to whether contractual relations exist. Moreover, the interests of the other participants in the course of business may be of the same value. It follows that it is reasonable that the actor only has to respect contractual relations known to him if at all.[39]

The level of protection of pure economic interests is even lower, as they rank last, are not clearly described and are not always obvious. Moreover, the risk of an unforeseeable number of claimants has to be considered. Therefore, the protection of pure economic interests only seems to be reasonable if there exists a special proximity between the persons concerned or the interests of the actor are of much less value and if he acts with the intent to cause damage. This means, for example, that the actor is not

---

33  *Cf.* under German law von Bar, 'Zur Bedeutung des Beweglichen Systems für die Dogmatik der Verkehrspflichten', in Bydlinski, Krejci, Schilcher and Steininger (Ed.), *Das bewegliche System im geltenden und künftigen Recht* (1986), p. 72 ff.; Münzberg, *Verhalten und Erfolg als Grundlagen der Rechtswidrigkeit und Haftung* (1966), p. 141 ff.

34  *See* Spier's report section VII.3.

35  *Cf.* Spier's report section VII.2.

36  *Cf.* under German law K. Scholz, *Der Begriff der Zumutbarkeit im Deliktsrecht* (1996).

37  *See* the reports on Case 10.

38  *See* the reports on Case 10.

39  *Cf.* the reports on Case 2. *See* the latest German discussion by Canaris, 'Der Schutz obligatorischer Forderungen nach § 823 Abs 1 BGB', *Steffen-Festschrift* (1995), p. 85; Medicus, 'Die Forderung als "sonstiges" Recht nach § 823 Abs 1 BGB?' *Steffen-Festschrift* (1995), p. 333; Becker, 'Schutz von Forderungen durch das Deliktsrecht?' AcP 196, 1996, 439.

allowed to cause pure economic loss by unfair competition, but he is allowed to do so by fair competition even with intent.

Above all, in establishing the violation of a duty of care one also has to consider whether the actor simply defended his object of legal protection against an unlawful attack (self-defence)[40] or whether he acted under necessity or because the help of the authorities could not be obtained in time (self-help) or with the approval of the injured person or by virtue of a licence.

Today, these grounds of justification are discussed separately. But they are only the result of weighing the interests in some typical situations[41] and a separate provision, therefore, is not necessary, nor is it desirable. This can be seen, for example, when self-defence is at stake: It is true that the unlawfulness of the attack is a very important factor, but not the only one to be considered. It is commonly recognized that the endangered interests of the person attacked and the interests of the assailant menaced by the self-defence must be taken into account and, therefore, in defending property of inferior value one is not allowed to kill or even wound the attacker seriously. By the same token, the consent of a person does not justify killing him.

In concluding, it should again be mentioned that interference with a clearly described, obvious and highly protected interest, e.g., the right to physical well-being or a right *in rem*, may indicate the violation of a duty of care.

# V. Subjective Fault

In the area of liability based on fault, responsibility of the actor may require not only violation of an objective duty to take care, but also subjective fault. Especially if the tortfeasor is mentally ill or a minor, he may not be culpable. Subjective fault may also be rejected if necessity is at stake. This topic still has to be discussed in greater depth.

It has to be pointed out that even if there is no subjective fault, the violation of a duty of care in combination with other factors may establish liability of the actor, e.g., if the consideration of the financial situation of both the wrongdoer and the injured person speaks in favour of liability of a mentally ill person.[42]

---

40    *Cf.* the reports on Case 8.

41    *Cf.* Widmer's (section II.B.1.) and Neethling's (section I.) report and also the report under Austrian law (section I.C.3). In this spirit under German law Münzberg, *Verhalten und Erfolg als Grundlagen der Rechtswidrig Keit und Haftung* (1996), p. 328 ff.; Fischer, *Die Rechtswidrigkeit* (1911), p. 192 ff.

42    *Cf.* the Austrian report section I.B.

# Index

*H. Koziol (ed.), Unification of Tort Law: Wrongfulness, 137–144.*
*©1998 Kluwer Law International. Printed in The Netherlands.*

**W**